Sacred TIME

"Christine Valters Paintner's vision deftly translates the seasons of the heart and cycles of the solar and lunar year into pathways of enlightenment and spiritual growth. As with the online experience out of which this book grew, *Sacred Time* is a rich feast of wisdom that encourages personal insights and a pilgrimage that leads us intentionally toward 'time out of time.'"

Moira Anne MacDermaid
Poet and Abbey of the Arts Sacred Time Jubilee participant

"In a season of life when time feels chaotic and uneven—sometimes slow, sometimes racing, sometimes monotonous, sometimes crazy—Christine Valters Paintner's book reminds me that I do not need to manage time but rather manage myself within the time that I am given: a time marked by cycles and seasons outside my control but beautiful and organic and awaiting my embrace. In *Sacred Time*, she eases me into a new appreciation for how God is at work in the mystery of time."

Ann M. Garrido
Associate Professor of Homiletics
Aquinas Institute of Theology

"In a world of increasing speed, work, and distraction, Christine Valters Paintner's *Sacred Time* is a welcome guide to shifting our spiritual gears into a mode of renewed attentiveness and intentionality. Beautifully written, this book helps readers adjust the rhythms of their lives to align more closely with that of God and creation."

Rev. Daniel P. Horan, O.F.M.
Duns Scotus Chair of Spirituality
Catholic Theological Union
Author of *The Franciscan Heart of Thomas Merton*

Sacred TIME

Embracing an Intentional Way of Life

Christine Valters Paintner

SORIN BOOKS  Notre Dame, IN

www.sorinbooks.com

Paperback: ISBN-13 978-1-932057-22-5

E-book: ISBN-13 978-1-932057-23-2

Cover image "Hopeful Promise" painting © 2019 by Betsy O'Neill, www.betsyoneillfineart.com.

Cover and text design by Andy Wagoner.

Printed and bound in the United States of America.

Library of Congress Cataloging-in-Publication Data
Names: Paintner, Christine Valters, author.
Title: Sacred time : embracing an intentional way of life / Christine
    Valters Paintner.
Description: Notre Dame, Indiana : Sorin Books, [2020] | Includes
    bibliographical references. | Summary: "In this book, Christine Valters
    Paintner guides readers in moving beyond their own lives and invites
    them to embrace the natural world and its rhythms that urge them toward
    rest, reflection, and growth"-- Provided by publisher.
Identifiers: LCCN 2020044658 | ISBN 9781932057225 (paperback) | ISBN
    9781932057232 (ebook)
Subjects: LCSH: Time--Religious aspects--Christianity.
Classification: LCC BT78 .P1555 2020 | DDC 248.2--dc23
LC record available at https://lccn.loc.gov/2020044658

She was someone who could not be rushed.
That seems like a small thing.
But it is actually a very amazing quality,
a very ancient one . . .
She went about her business
as if she could live forever,
and forever was very, very long.

—Alice Walker, *The Temple of My Familiar*

Contents

Acknowledgments

My favorite part of the writing process is enjoying the long, quiet days when I can lose myself in a subject. I have the gift of largely being able to structure my time in spacious and life-giving ways, and these stretches and generous margins to my days, as Thoreau once wrote, are integral to my creativity continuing to flourish.

As always I offer deep gratitude to my husband, John, with whom I delightedly live my moments, days, weeks, months, and years and who also works alongside me in this ministry. I love spanning time together.

I want to express special thanks to the Hosking House Trust, a wonderful organization in Clifford Chambers, England, that offers space and time for women to write. I had the gift of spending time there in February 2020 when I was completing this manuscript, and the uninterrupted time as well as the lovely cottage provided were an enormous support.

I continue to count myself incredibly lucky and blessed to be able to work with the fine editors and team at Ave Maria Press, who offer wonderful support for all the ideas I bring to them and make the process of bringing a book into the world a pleasure.

Finally, gratitude goes both to my Benedictine community and to our Abbey of the Arts members, whose commitment to savoring, slowness, and spaciousness is a balm in this frenzied world.

Introduction

> The closer we are to the productions of time—that is, to
> the eternal—the more easily we understand the particu-
> lar currents we must navigate on any given day.
>
> —David Whyte,
> *Crossing the Unknown Sea: Work as a Pilgrimage of Identity*

We live in a breathless world.

Everything around us seems to move at faster and faster speeds, summoning us to keep up. We multitask, we organize, we simplify; we do all we can to keep on top of the many demands on our time. We yearn for a day with more hours in it so we can complete all we long to do.

We often talk about wasted time, time spent like money, or time fleeting. This rushed and frenzied existence is not sacred time. Sacred time is time governed by the rhythms of creation, rhythms that incorporate times of rest as essential to our own unfolding. Sacred time is time spent being present to the moments of eternity available to us whenever we choose to pause and breathe.

In sacred time, we step out of the madness of our lives and choose to reflect, linger, savor, and slow down. We gain new perspective here. We have all had those moments of time outside of time when we felt as if we were touching eternity, bathed in a different kind of rhythm. Touching eternity brings cohesion to our lives and reminds us of the goodness and surplus of living because it honors the rhythms of the soul.

The clock with its forced march is not the only marker of time. Our calendars with their five- and ten-year strategic plans rob us of our future as we desperately try to cram things in. Each slow, mindful breath, the rising and setting of the sun, the expansion and contraction of the moon, the ripening and releasing of the seasons—these all mark a different quality of time and invite us into a deepened and renewed way of being.

Psychologist Mihaly Csikszentmihalyi has written extensively about our "flow state,"[1] that experience of moving beyond consciousness of time's ticking and into a place of timelessness. Wisdom traditions tell us that reaching these states of spaciousness and ease takes time, but time is the one thing that feels most scarce, and so we seek quick-and-easy fixes to our time anxiety. Often this includes rushing more, sleeping less, and being distracted by the multiple demands on our attention.

Gary Eberle, in his book *Sacred Time and the Search for Meaning*, writes:

> Sacred time is what we experience when we step outside the quick flow of life and luxuriate, as it were, in a realm where there is enough of everything, where we are not trying to fill a void in ourselves or the world, where we exist for a moment at both the deepest and the loftiest levels of our existence and participate in the eternal life of all that is. In simpler, or perhaps just slower, times, people seemed to enter this realm more regularly, or perhaps even to live with one foot inside it. Prayer, meditation, religious rituals, and holy days provided gateways into eternity that allowed us to return to the world of daily time refreshed and renewed, with an understanding that beneath the busyness of daily life there was an underpinning of calm, peace, and sufficiency.[2]

This is one of the functions of religious tradition and practice: to give us tools that help us cross the threshold into liminal space and time, outside of ordinary rhythms.

Eberle goes on to write that we experience time both horizontally and vertically:

> The horizontal takes us along a straight line from past to future. This is what allows us to plan events and schedule meetings. It is the time we measure with clocks. The other way of experiencing time, the vertical, seems to deliver us from the flow of horizontal time. In moments of rapture, deep meditation, dream states, or intense celebration, we feel liberated from time's passing. The clock does not stop, of course, but we do not hear it ticking. When we connect with vertical time, we step out of horizontal time and touch eternity.[3]

Our clocks and calendars were created as tools to serve us, but the roles have reversed, and now we serve them in their perpetual drive forward. They measure time horizontally, in a linear way, always ticking off the missed moments. For some, the calculations are literal with productivity expectations rising and the need to produce more and more in the same amount of time. Our schedules are so packed full of appointments and commitments that there is no time to lose ourselves in dreaming, wandering, and playing or in the eternal now.

It is only when we move more slowly and with intention that we can touch the vertical modes of experiencing time. In this book we will see how the slow witness of the natural world and its rhythms offers us a portal into another experience of time and offers ways to begin practicing this alternate way of being.

When we look at the world around us, at nature and creation, we find exquisite examples of sacred timing. I've witnessed the monarch butterflies resting in Cape May, New Jersey, in the midst of their migration. I've seen cherry trees blossoming each April in Seattle, Washington, around the building where I lived. I've enjoyed the salmon festival in the Pacific Northwest celebrating their return each autumn. And now living in Ireland, I've welcomed the salmon home to Lough Corrib after they've crossed the Atlantic to return to the place of their origins to spawn and die. I've been in the Arctic Circle in Norway just before their two months of polar darkness began, and what I found most surprising and refreshing was how the restaurants and cafés didn't have bright lights to try to dispel the darkness. Instead, everything was lit with candles; there was a sense of welcoming winter's gifts.

Seasons such as winter call for hibernation and rest, moving into darkness and mystery. Yet we are bombarded with a ubiquitous call to shop endlessly and to socialize as much as possible, while lights are strung everywhere to stave off the night. This now begins as early as late summer, and at least by Halloween. Rather than trying to keep the brightness of summer throughout the year, I suggest that we look at time as a spiral—through the lens of each breath's rise and fall, the rhythms of the sun and moon, and the longer cycles of a lifetime, generations, and the universe itself.

In his book *World Enough and Time,* author Christian McEwen writes about how consumerism even affects how we approach the soulful activities of our lives:

> Meanwhile, we talk of saving/wasting/investing/buying time as if life itself were just another form of currency. We turn Carl Honoré's *In Praise of Slowness* into a surprise bestseller; we crowd into poetry readings by Mary Oliver and Naomi Shihab Nye. We play soothing ocean music before we go to sleep, and get up early to practice yoga and meditation. We turn our earnest purposeful consumer-oriented brains to slowness and creativity as if they too could be added to our current shopping list, and paid for with our gold American Express card.[4]

Of course, ultimately we are unable to purchase contentment, despite what advertising would tell us. Many folks are using mindfulness as a productivity tool rather than a way to challenge a culture that speeds its way ahead. Contemplative practices become ways to cope with a relentless world of work and busyness. Poetry and yoga get squeezed in between all the other things we need to do.

Cultural Perspectives

I am a woman planted firmly in middle age, aware of my mortality in ways I wasn't in my teens, twenties, thirties, and even forties. I am also someone who, for the last twenty years, has embraced a path rooted in monastic practice, especially the Christian desert, Celtic, and Benedictine traditions. I find the way of the monk to be an alternative to our contemporary culture. The wisdom from the Christian traditions I follow gives me the courage I need to live more mindfully, more intentionally, more slowly, and more attentively than I would otherwise. Through these traditions, I am connected to a whole lineage of people who cherish time and its gifts.

I have also lived in different cultures with different perspectives on time, beginning with my childhood upbringing in the heart of midtown Manhattan, with its endless rush and bustle, and eventually moving to California in my twenties and to Seattle in my thirties. Each move represented a gradual slowing down, as each culture offered a different approach to the madness of modern life. Now in my forties and fifties, I am settling into life in Galway, a city on the west coast of Ireland, where "Irish time" is very distant from my urban upbringing. I love the slowness of life here and the less exacting schedules. The whole attitude toward life is much more relaxed than what I have previously experienced.

I am also a woman who loves nature and the wisdom I discover there. Forests and oceans call me by name. I feel most alive in these places where there are no clocks, just the changing quality of light. My practice of yoga introduced me to the wonders of the breath. The monastic tradition of praying the Hours plunged me into a heightened appreciation of the texture of each day's unfolding.

A dear friend in Seattle who is a rabbi introduced me to the incredible gift that is the Sabbath. As I grow older, I have grown in my appreciation of the moon and her cycles through the sky. The night sky teaches me about a more expansive time. And when my mother died in 2003, I learned to love the whole circle of seasons as I moved through my own release and grief and slowly back toward blossoming and fruit again. I fell in love with the possibilities of winter and darkness as time for dreaming and imagining, for not rushing anymore but allowing deep rest.

Chronos and *Kairos*

The Greek myths may help us understand this dual relationship we have to time, which can be destructive and life-giving. In the ancient story the Greek god Chronos was cursed: he would one day be overthrown by one of his children. So each time a child of his was born, he would devour the child to prevent the curse from taking place. He is depicted with a scythe and is known as the god of agriculture. Later he became associated with time and its devouring and destructive aspects. *Chronos* became the name for the kind of time that makes us keenly aware of its passing, always moving us inevitably toward our own ends.

In *World Enough and Time*, McEwen writes:

> When the Lilliputians first saw Gulliver's watch, that "wonderful kind of engine . . . a globe, half silver and half of some transparent metal [glass!]," they told themselves it had to be his god. After all, "he very seldom did anything without consulting it: he called it his oracle, and said it pointed out the time for every action of his life."[5]

We have clocks everywhere now: on our computer screens and phones, in our cars and on our microwaves. They hover above us at airports and train stations, urging us to rush to keep up with the schedule. As sociologist Juliet Schor points out in an article in *Yes!* magazine, we "work too much, eat too quickly, socialize too little, drive and sit in traffic for too many hours, don't get enough sleep, and feel harried too much of the time."[6]

Meanwhile, there is another kind of time, one that is more life-giving. The Greeks also had a word for the more life-giving aspects of time: *Kairos*. Kairos is known as the god of opportunity and is depicted with wings. Time may be the destroyer of things, but it is also the medium through which creativity happens. Time can be life-giving when we view it from an alternate perspective: that of touching eternity.

Author Jay Griffiths writes in *A Sideways Look at Time* that Chronos "gives his name to absolute time, linear, chronological and quantifiable. But the Greeks had another, far more slippery colorful, god of time, Kairos. Kairos was the god of tim*ing*, of opportunity, of chance and mischance, of different aspects of time, the auspicious and not-so-auspicious. Time qualitative."[7] When we eat and sleep because we are hungry and tired, that is *Kairos* time; if we do so because the clock tells us it is the time to do so, that is *Chronos* time.

Kairos is the time we experience on retreat, when the pressures of the world recede and there is just this moment now beckoning for attention. We are in *Kairos* time when we are with a loved one, immersed in laughter and meaningful conversation, and we lose track of what time it is. We experience *Kairos* time when we are in the flow of creating and we forget even to look at our watches or phones for a while.

The Wheel of Time

How do we open ourselves to *Kairos* more often? How do we pause on the horizontal progression of time and touch the vertical moments of eternity? I believe part of the answer is opening ourselves to a connection to cyclical and spiral understandings of time such as we have in nature. Much of Christian monastic practice and tradition is rooted in this understanding and relationship.

Several years ago I went away for a retreat by myself for a week. I rented a cottage on Saltspring Island, which is one of the Gulf Islands in British Columbia. I had been on many retreats before, but they were usually a guided program at a retreat center with a facilitator and schedule to follow. This time, I was alone.

When I went on this retreat, I was feeling a deeper call to solitude and found myself in this place by the sea long enough to really sink into my own internal rhythms. I started listening more deeply to myself in those quiet days. I began to experience a profound freedom to attend to my body's needs as they arose—for food, for rest, for movement, for stillness.

What I discovered in those days away was that my spirituality thrives when I can allow it to be organic—when I create enough space to respond to what the day offers. I am someone who loves to plan and make lists, and yet what is most life-giving for me in the overall arc of my life is to listen deeply to what my life is calling me toward and to shape my life in response.

There is a beautiful rhythm of rise and fall found in every breath we take, the rising and setting of the sun each day, the balance between work and Sabbath time each week, the waxing and waning of the moon each month, the flowering and releasing of the earth through her seasons, the seasons of our lifetimes, and the larger rhythms of ancestral and cosmic time.

In the Celtic tradition, time is depicted as a wheel, as in many other indigenous traditions, always turning and moving through the cycles of seasons. The Christian liturgical calendar is similarly immersed in cycles. These seasons reflect inner movements as well, in which we are invited into ritual to mark the new moments. Rituals immerse us in liminal space and time, which is time outside of time. We touch the eternal moment. Ritual creates a holy pause and connects us to the very rhythm of the world that sustains us, reminding us of the slow unfolding and ripening of things. Ritual, whether religious or otherwise, connects us to a deep source, a well of refreshment.

We don't have to go anywhere in particular to experience sacred time. We don't have to give up our lives in the world and run off to a monastery to be immersed in the holiness of time's unfolding. Really what we are invited to is a shift in perspective. Think of those optical illusions where you look at a drawing and see one thing but, when you shift your gaze, you see something else entirely. Experiencing sacred time can be as accessible as allowing our perspective to shift.

Catholic philosopher Josef Pieper, in his book *In Tune with the World*, writes about festivals as an essential aspect of sacred time, and he describes how they function as a kind of wealth, not of money, but of "existential richness."[8] Entering into sacred time requires us to embrace leisure, which is different from what the medieval monks warned against in sloth. Sloth led to restlessness and agitation. To experience true leisure we must enter fully into the invitation each moment offers us and experience the free, surplus gifts of time. We enter through prayer, meditation, ritual, and celebration—through the practice of paying attention and opening ourselves to the possibility that eternity dwells with us now.

Speed encourages the great urge to escape from ourselves to nowhere in particular, some imagined better existence. Multitasking means we are doing many things with poor attention and grinding ourselves down in the process. Slow time, on the other hand, means we dip into an overflowing well that exists beneath the surface of daily life and into which we can plunge again and again to quench our thirsty hearts. By aligning ourselves with the rhythms of the seasons, we connect to something much larger than simply us. We experience a cohesion of time between us and our community, which includes the wider community of nature and creation.

Crossing the Threshold

The seasons—whether of the breath, day, week, month, year, lifetime, generations, or cosmos—invite us into a profound respect for thresholds. In our usual day-to-day awareness, one moment isn't especially different from another. In seasonal time, we become aware of the continual invitation to cross a threshold into a deeper awareness. Dawn, day, dusk, and dark each carry different qualities and questions. Spring, summer, fall, and winter each offer new perspectives on the rhythms of life.

Thresholds are what the Celts called "thin places," where heaven and earth seem nearer to one another. A threshold is a place between, where we are invited into not knowing what the next moment will bring. Of course, we never really do know what life will bring us, but we often march through our days with a sense of sameness and tedium.

Seasonal time can give us a profound appreciation of the varying textures of our lives. We honor that the current moment is different than what came before. Perhaps you are at a place in your life of discerning a new direction and find yourself at your own threshold.

Let us focus on embracing a different experience of time: Time as unfolding rather than always running away from us. Time as offering invitations rather than demands that we keep up. Eternal time, present moment time, the fullness of time.

Sacred time is time devoted to the heart, to things that matter, to wonder and beauty, to catching glimpses of eternity. Sacred time is measured not in minutes or hours but in moments and spans, offering us an inner sense of expansiveness.

Overview of the Book

There are eight chapters to this book. I begin with the rhythms of the breath and slowly expand through the hours of the day, weekly Sabbath, monthly lunar cycles, seasonal rhythms, seasons of a lifetime, ancestral time, and cosmic time. Each offers an opening into becoming more present to the eternal moment where time expands and offers its gifts to us. Each is centered on the rhythms of rise and fall, fullness and emptiness, expansion and contraction, and movement and stillness.

Each chapter of this book has five sections. First is my reflection on the theme, followed by a scripture reflection from my dear husband, John Valters Paintner. Then you are invited into experiential explorations through a meditation and a creative practice. The chapter closes with a blessing in the form of a poem I wrote for each aspect of time. You are always invited to write your own poem as well to explore the textures and contours of the chapter's theme.

As with many of the books I write, but perhaps this one in particular due to its theme, I recommend moving slowly through it. Read one chapter per week or even per month, and really make space to explore that aspect of time in your own life. Gathering with a friend or two, or in a small group, is another wonderful way to deepen into these practices and ways of being in the world.

I believe that our rushed, overly productive lives, which try to extract value from all of our minutes, are intimately tied to our disconnection from the natural world and seeing it as a resource to be exploited, rather than as a wise guide and teacher of healing rhythms. My deepest prayer is that we might slow our rushed lives to a tempo that brings us alive so that we have time to be present to the wondrous gifts available to us in each moment.

ONE

The Breath

To breathe deeply and gently is to draw near this Spirit, to feel oneself inhaled and exhaled by God.

—Jean-Yves Leloup,
Being Still: Reflections on an Ancient Mystical Tradition

We begin this journey through the layers of sacred time with the most organic and primal of units—the breath. Certainly there are shorter and more defined time spans, such as the second and even milli- or nano-second, but these are not particularly meaningful in terms of our human experience. Genesis tells us we were breathed into by God and given life. Psalm 104 proclaims God as the sustainer of life. And in the book of Ezekiel, the dry bones are reanimated, made alive again, through the gift of breath.

Our breath continues automatically whether we're conscious of it or not. The breath is a threshold—a gateway to a profound immersion in this moment here and now. When we cultivate the ability to allow our breath to anchor us, our awareness can become deeply rooted in the present. The past has come to completion; the future is yet to be created. And while both remembering and dreaming are vital acts, when they move into regret and anxiety, we are drained of the life offered to us right now. Breath invites us to be here. Someone who lives to be eighty years old will take close to 700 million breaths in their lifetime, on average, so there are many opportunities offered to us to step across the threshold into an experience of being more present to our lives. The more rushed and restless we feel, the more we are invited to pause and taste eternity by paying attention to this moment in time.

We've all had experiences when the clock drags on and we wish our time away, or when the clock feels relentless in its onward march with never enough hours to get things done. The key is not to multitask so we

1

can be more productive. The breath teaches us that the key is actually to do the opposite—to learn to solo-task, to focus on what is at hand, to slow down. The breath can help us with this.

How many of us have lamented that there just aren't enough hours in the day? Yet how many of us have also lost track of time and touched those eternal moments when listening to a piece of beautiful music, having a conversation with a friend, strolling through a magical place, writing a poem, or gardening? These moments of time outside of time are often what bring meaning to our lives.

With each breath we inhale oxygen and exhale carbon dioxide, while the trees do the reverse in what Teilhard de Chardin called "the breathing together of all things."[1] Philosopher and ecologist David Abram reminds us of the sustaining power of sacred breath in Hebrew cosmology when he writes that "sacred breath enters not just into human beings . . . it also animates and sustains the whole of the sensible world. . . . Without the continual outflow of God's breath, all of the letters that stand within the things of this world—all the letter combinations embodied in particular animals, plants, and stones—would be extinguished."[2] The poet Mary Oliver asks the question, "Listen—are you breathing just a little and calling it a life?"[3] which opens us to the possibility that deepening our breath is also a deepening of life and our presence to our own aliveness.

Fighting time and forever feeling its scarcity is a sure way to reach the end of each day and our lives feeling exhausted, frustrated, depleted, and perhaps cheated out of time. The monks and hermits of various spiritual traditions know this truth—that rushing does not bring the grace of the fullness of time; only slowing down can do that. This is the paradox at the heart of contemplative life. When we slow down, life and its possibilities seem to expand. When we rush, everything feels constricted. It is in bringing ourselves even more fully to the present moment that we begin to see that eternity isn't a faraway reality behind the pearly gates. Eternity is right here below the surface of things; and we can access it—through both our own intention and our practice—and allow ourselves to be taken over by it, surrendering to the flow of spaciousness and ease that we occasionally touch without even trying.

Remember Your Mortality

Sometimes our resistance to slowness is because we fear what we'll encounter within ourselves when we slow our busy, distracted minds enough to listen to what is happening deep within: the shadows that have gone untended, the regrets we feel, or the sorrow over time spent on things that weren't our great loves in the world. The reality of our mortality is a core aspect of our relationship to time and our sense of time running out. The ancient monks had a practice of *memento mori*—to remember your death, or to "keep death daily before your eyes," as St. Benedict writes in his Rule. This was not a morbid exercise, but a practice of gratitude for the gift of life, the gift of awareness in this moment now.

St. Francis referred to death as "Sister Death" in his Canticle of Creation, a companion and kin on the path of our lives to remind us of the treasure each breath brings. Each breath we are given is another opportunity to fall even more in love with the world. Each breath is a doorway to the eternal.

One of my most sacred memories is sitting with my mother as she lay dying in the intensive care unit at a hospital in Sacramento, California. Each breath was monitored along with her heartbeat. She had a ventilator so she wouldn't choke to death, but all of her systems were shutting down while I sat vigil with her for five days. It was like being in time outside of time. Everything fell away. I did not concern myself with my teaching or other responsibilities; anything that was not absolutely necessary was released, forgotten for the duration. My husband flew down to be with me, and other family members joined us. We waited, we sang to her, we anointed her; we took turns catching fistfuls of sleep, nibbling on snacks, breathing sometimes slowly and deeply and sometimes in great heaving sobs. We continued to wait until her very final exhale came and the machine had one long, sustained beep, her chest lay flat and still, and I began to wail.

Breath can be an ally in labor or when we experience physical or emotional pain. In the terrible grief that followed my mother's death, sometimes all that carried me through was my breath—getting through the next five breaths, then the next five.

Midwives coach women in labor over when and how to breathe to facilitate birthing. Spiritual directors and soul friends offer a similar guidance for those who are birthing something new in their lives at a soul level or those who are moving through a season of grieving. There can be impatience and anxiety, and the breath helps us to stay with the process, be present to the unfolding, and release our need to see what is coming and the exact shape of things.

Memento mori offers us the tremendous gift of reminding us that our breaths are limited. That reminder confronts us with the vital question: Knowing we won't live forever, how will we choose to live now? Forever harried, frazzled, and anxious, or in a slow, reverent way as much as possible?

Scripture Reflection from John Valters Paintner

Story of Adam and Eve
(Genesis 2:4-25)

> In the day that the LORD God made the earth and the heavens, when no plant of the field was yet in the earth and no herb of the field had yet sprung up—for the LORD God had not caused it to rain upon the earth, and there was no one to till the ground; but a stream would rise from the earth, and water the whole face of the ground—then the LORD God formed man from the dust of the ground, and breathed into his nostrils the breath of life; and the man became a living being.
>
> —Genesis 2:4b-7

The Irish language is full of proverbs, and one of my favorites is *Tús maith, leath na hoibre*, which translates into English as "A good start is half the work." It's practical advice from a largely agrarian culture. Crops and livestock keep their own schedules. And procrastination only breeds more work later. It's best to get up early and get "tucked in," as they say. Why wait? And so that is what we are doing here now: starting at the beginning.

In terms of the presented order of scripture, this is not the first of the creation myths. However, it is commonly believed to have been written first, with chapter 1 of Genesis being added later. Now, both creation myths are important (even if the details and order of events in each contradict one another), and the sequence of the two stories also matters greatly.

In chapter 1, we learn of a good and loving God who creates an abundant and orderly world out of the chaos. God is almost methodical in creation. One thing leads to another, all with a purpose. Once everything is prepared, according to the grand design, humans are created in God's likeness. And it was very good.

Chapters 2 and 3 teach us that we humans are to blame for why God's perfect creation is no longer perfect: the existence of suffering, pain, death, and so forth. The how and why of that isn't relevant to this discussion today. But this second creation myth picks up from where the first one ends: a good and loving God carefully makes the world, including humans.

In this second myth, humans are the first living things created. We are told here that God formed us carefully and artistically from the earth. We were molded, crafted into being. But that was just our form. What gave us life, according to this story, was that God breathed life into us. Our being was filled with God's Spirit. Breathing was the first thing we did. It was an extension, a continuation, of God's creative act, and it is a sign of God's divinity within each and every one of us.

Which brings us to our theme—breath. Or more to the point, it brings us to the rhythm and cycle of breathing, the in and out, the holding and releasing, the filling and emptying. We could begin anywhere on this wheel of breath, but this passage from scripture lays out an example for us. And so to paraphrase Genesis, chapter 2, "God breathed into our nostrils the breath of life and we became living beings."

- With every inhale, remember that life is gift, graced from our Creator. All good things are given to us from a good and loving God.

- Pause, filled with gratitude, and be filled with the Spirit of God. The Creator is all around us, but also within, filling our being.

- Then, with gratitude, breathe out, sharing the gift freely given to us with others. We join in the creative act when we give to one another.

- And so pause again, resting into the emptiness. Acknowledge the need to stop and rest, before we can be ready to begin again.

Set aside time each day to take even just a moment to concentrate on your breathing and make it a prayer of gratitude.

Practice: Slow Being

Time is not the steady beat of a clock, nor is eternity an experience of complete stillness. We actually experience time in various tempos. Think of our bodies with their various rhythms. The heartbeat and breath are the two most foundational, the ones we can hear and connect with in an intimate way. When we sleep, our breath slows way down, and when we run or walk up a hill, our breath speeds up. When we experience strong emotion such as fear, anxiety, or joy, our heart rate increases and breath often becomes faster and shallower. When we meditate we can slow these down again.

St. Hildegard of Bingen, a twelfth-century German Benedictine abbess, described herself as a "feather on the breath of God."[4] I love this image. There is such delicacy in being a feather, a sense of being carried gently. She also saw the breath as what gives the body life, just as the air is what gives the earth life. We can join together with other creatures, trees, and plants in an extravagant harmony of breath.

Each chapter of this book will invite you into a practice of slowing down in some way. Your first practice is to try something simple: five slow, deep breaths. See if you can keep your awareness focused on each inhale and exhale. Notice when your mind starts to wander away. Allow yourself a few moments to rest into the experience of being inhaled and exhaled by God. As you sink into this place of rhythm and stillness, what do you notice about your own longings? If you imagine on the inhale that you are being filled with the energy and wisdom needed to share your gifts, and on the exhale that you are offering them in service to the world, what images come to your mind and heart? What quality does time take on? Do you notice yourself still rushed and frenzied, or is another perspective offered?

Statio is the monastic practice of blessing the in-between moments. We get so impatient when appointments run behind and cause a cascading effect of delays from one commitment to another. Or we stand in line absentmindedly filling the time with mindless scrolling through social media, which rarely does much to uplift us. What if we instead allowed those in-between moments to offer us the chance for five slow, deep breaths? Before you hop out of the car to another task, slow yourself way down. Embrace the in-between moment.

We live in a culture that values productivity and achievement at the expense of our physical and emotional health, our time for relationships and creative pursuits, and our time to simply savor and cherish the gifts each moment might bring. The breath is a gateway into this awareness, with its ability to slow us down so we can experience time in a different way, deepen into friendship with eternity, and grow familiar with the experience of spaciousness in our lives and learn to cherish it.

The breath offers us another gift. Often when we are rushing through life, our whole physical system is running on adrenaline; cortisol pulses through us, our breathing is shallow, and our muscles tense to brace us for what comes next. These are some of the reasons it can actually be physically uncomfortable to slow down if it is not our usual practice. Our bodies are so primed for action and can feel a profound restlessness as we try to stop that pattern. By working with the breath in an intentional way, we can impact these biological responses to stress, which keep us amped up all the time. We can begin to slow our systems down so we feel more at ease with pausing.

Modern life seems to move at full speed, and many of us can hardly catch our breath between the demands of earning a living, nurturing family and friendships, and the hundreds of small daily details, such as paying our bills, cleaning, and grocery shopping. More and more we feel stretched thin by commitments and lament our busyness, but without a clear sense of the alternative. Even when there is nothing immediately upcoming on our schedules, we are overwhelmed by all the things we feel we should do. There is no space left to consider other options, and heading off on a retreat to ponder new possibilities may be beyond our reach.

But there are opportunities for breathing spaces within our days. The monastic tradition invites us into the practice of stopping one thing before beginning another. Doing so acknowledges that in the space of transition and threshold is a sacred dimension, a holy pause full of possibility. What might it be like to allow a five-minute window to sit in silence between appointments? Or to take five long, slow, deep breaths after finishing a phone call or checking your email and before pushing on to the next thing?

We often think of these in-between times as wasted moments and inconveniences rather than opportunities to return again and again to the present, to awaken to the gifts right here, not the ones we imagine waiting for us beyond the next door. But what if we built in these thresholds between our daily activities, just for a few minutes, to intentionally savor silence and breath?

When we pause between activities or moments in our day, we open ourselves to the possibility of discovering a new kind of presence in the in-between times. When we rush from one thing to another, we skim over the surface of life, losing that sacred attentiveness that brings forth revelations in the most ordinary of moments.

We are continually crossing thresholds in our lives—both the literal thresholds when moving through doorways, leaving the building, or going to another room and the metaphorical thresholds when time becomes a transition space of waiting and tending. We hope for news about a friend struggling with illness; we are longing for clarity about our own deepest dreams. This *place between* is a place of stillness, where we let go of what came before and prepare ourselves to enter fully into what comes next.

Meditation: The Seasons of the Breath

As you pause during the day to breathe, imagine as you inhale that you are breathing in the Spirit. The Latin word for "spirit" is *spiritus* and is the root of the word "inspire"; when you inhale, you breathe in the Spirit's inspiring and enlivening presence. Allow that moment of fullness to connect you with the sacred presence always sustaining you. When you exhale, imagine releasing what is not needed in this moment, setting aside all that keeps you from God. Notice how your perspective on time shifts when you pay attention to your breath.

I credit my practice of yoga over the last twenty-five years for my understanding of the ways breath can help me be present to my experience and lift me out of the relentless anxiety of my mind around having enough time. When I breathe deeply not only do I discover an anchor into this moment here and now but also there is a physiological effect on my body that calms my nervous system and allows me to be more present. When I slow myself down and tend to the breath, I discover a fullness I didn't see before in my rushed existence.

I used to think of the breath as only the inhale and exhale, but in my yoga classes I was taught *sama vritti*, which is known as "equal parts breathing." You begin by allowing the inhale and the exhale to have the same length; for example, breathe in for a count of three and breathe out for a count of three. Once you've established that steady rhythm, you add another layer to the practice—breathe in for three, hold the fullness for three, exhale for three, hold the emptiness for three. Those moments between the inhale and exhale and between the exhale and inhale don't often receive our attention, but they do offer us windows into the experience of fullness and emptiness that arrives with each breath.

I began to see how this four-part breathing rhythm actually reflects the four-part rhythm of the seasons with their movements of blossoming (inhale), fruitfulness (hold), release (exhale), and resting (hold). We experience it during the day as well with the four hinges of dawn, day, dusk, and dark and in the lunar cycles of waxing, fullness, waning, and darkness. Why is this important? I've found that the more I live into an awareness of this four-part sacred rhythm at the heart of everything—the more I see and experience the rise and fall, the fullness and emptiness of each breath—the more I grow in trust that when I am invited into release and rest in my life, flowering and fruitfulness will eventually follow.

The following is a simple meditation for paying attention to the different qualities of the breath. Begin by getting in a comfortable position and closing your eyes if you would like. Then pay attention to your breath without changing anything. Simply take a few moments to connect with this life-sustaining energy moving through you.

Now start to slow your breath down and move into an awareness of the four parts of the breath—the moment of inhale, the pause between your inhale and exhale, the moment of exhale, and the pause between your exhale and inhale. Take a couple of breaths, focusing your awareness on all four moments in your breath and noticing the different quality each part has. We're going to spend a little bit of time exploring each of these four moments.

As you breathe, bring your focus to your inhalation and allow it to be slow and full. As you repeat each breath cycle, notice how that moment of breathing in and taking in oxygen feels in your body. Call to mind the dawn as a time of awakening, an experience of breathing in new life. Feel the experience of spring's blossoming in your body. Hold this question: How are you being invited to awaken today? Take a few moments of silence to simply experience the fullness of your inhalation.

Now, as you continue noticing your breath, bring your focus to the moment between your inhalation and your exhalation. Pause for just a moment between the inhale and exhale, and notice how this moment of the breath feels in your body. Experience the fullness of oxygen in your lungs. With each breath cycle, pause at this moment and call to mind the height of the day as a time of fullness. Feel the experience of summer's heat and fruitfulness in your body. Hold this question: How are you being invited into the fullness of who you are today? Take a few moments of silence to simply experience this moment between inhale and exhale.

Continue to notice your breath, but now bring your focus to your exhalation and allow it to be slow and full. As you repeat each breath cycle, notice how that moment of breathing out feels in your body; sink into the experience of surrender and release that exhaling invites us into. With each exhale, call to mind dusk as a time of letting go, an experience of releasing that which no longer serves you, of being confronted with your own mortality and the knowledge that one day you will release your final exhale. Feel the experience of autumn's vulnerability in your body. Hold this question: What are you being asked to release today? Take a few moments of silence to simply experience the surrender of your exhalation.

Now move to the final part of the breath. As you continue your breath cycles, bring your focus to the moment between exhalation and inhalation, and pause there for a moment with each breath. Experience the emptiness of breath as it leaves your body and you await that next inhale. Allow yourself to rest for a moment in that place of discomfort and unknowing. As you repeat each breath cycle, notice how that moment of the emptiness of breath feels in your body. Call to mind the night as a time of darkness and unknowing, a time of resting and waiting. Feel the experience of winter's call to rest in your body. Hold this question: How are you being invited to be still today? Take a few moments of silence to simply experience this moment between exhale and inhale.

Now return to your normal breath pattern and simply notice how your body is feeling. Take a few moments to see if you can bring awareness of the full cycle of your breath—allow all four parts to have a moment of pause and awareness. Move through the seasons of spring, summer, autumn, and winter with each breath. Move through the hours of the day with each breath. Simply experience the rise and fall in your body, knowing that this is the rhythm at the heart of creation as well.

I invite you in the days ahead to take just a few minutes each day to practice this breath awareness and see what it has to teach you. Notice which moments of the breath feel more at ease and which ones stretch you open in new ways.

Creative Exploration: Create a Breath Prayer

Yogic tradition recognizes the power of the breath to shift our bodies, our energy, and our emotions. There are a multitude of breath practices to balance, stimulate, or relax. We often think of breath work as the provenance of Eastern traditions, but in the early Christian Church, too, the breath was a powerful way of praying.

The desert monks had various ways of praying with the in-breath and the out-breath as an anchor for their awareness and to continually turn their attention to God. Orthodox theologian Jean-Yves Leloup writes, "To be attentive to every inhalation and exhalation can take us very far. In the hesychastic tradition awareness of the breath is a true spiritual practice. The breath is *ruah*, the breath of God, the *pneuma*, which we call the Holy Spirit."[5]

In the early Christian church, monks developed a form of breath prayer to help them abide by St. Paul's call to "pray without ceasing" (1

Thes 5:17). Because our breath is an ongoing companion, the monks realized that by connecting our prayers with our breath we can let our breath become one continual prayer to the Divine. The practice they developed was to take a short excerpt from the scriptures and breathe in with the first part of the text and breathe out with the second. This was repeated again and again, forming a kind of mantra prayer in which the words and breath blended together to keep the monk's attention focused on God. The most common text at the time was "Lord Jesus Christ, Son of God, have mercy on me, a sinner," but you can choose any passage or phrase that shimmers or enlivens your heart.

In my book *The Wisdom of the Body*, I introduce this practice in its traditional form of tying the words to the inhale and the exhale.[6] Because here we are exploring the four parts of the breath, I invite you to consider creating a phrase that you could tie to the inhale, pause for fullness, exhale, and pause for emptiness.

You can choose a phrase from scripture that has meaning for you or another phrase that you are drawn to. Here are some suggestions:

- Let everything that has breath praise God! (See Psalm 150:6.)
- Look! I am going to put breath into you and make you live again! (See Ezekiel 37:5.)
- Truly my soul finds rest in God; my salvation comes from God. (See Psalm 62:1.)
- The peace of God, which transcends all understanding. (See Philippians 4:7.)
- Come to me, all you who are weary, and I will give you rest. (See Matthew 11:28.)

See if you can divide the passage into four sections in a way that feels somewhat natural to your breath pattern. Here's an example:

- Inhale: Come to me, all you
- Pause for fullness: who are weary,
- Exhale: and I will give you
- Pause for emptiness: rest

If working with the traditional pattern of inhale and exhale works better for you, feel free to adapt the prayer for your needs. You can also take a line of poetry and use that as your prayer practice instead.

Make time each day to pause, maybe setting your alarm on your phone as a chime to remind you four times during the day to enter into this breath prayer for a minute or two and notice its effect on your body and spirit.

Closing Blessing

Breath by breath we move through a life. The breath can be a gateway to eternity here and now. At the end of our lives, will we feel more satisfied with a list of achievements or with a series of deeply lived moments when we were able to step outside of time and breathe in the fullness of our lives? What do you discover when you slow your breathing down? What new portals of awareness open into your life?

Breath

This
breathing
in is a miracle,
this breathing out, release,
this breathing in a welcome to
the unseen gifts which sustain me each
moment, this breathing out a sweet sigh,
a bow to my mortality, this breathing in
a holy yes to life, this breathing out
a sacred no to all that causes
me to clench and gasp,
this breathing in is a
revelation, this
breathing out,
freedom.[7]

TWO

Rhythms of the Day

> The rhythm of day is the rhythm of fire, the tiny flame, dawn of the dawn, birds rubbing their beaks together to make a spark of morning, the roaring teenage fire of noon, the mature fire of afternoon and on, on, the sun walks on, to the low heart-fire of evening, grandfather fire and grandmother ash.
>
> —Jay Griffiths, *Savage Grace: A Journey in Wildness*

I have lived in a number of different cities over the course of my life so far. Growing up in Manhattan, the world often felt quite rushed. I walked fast along sidewalks and felt impatient with those who didn't. Subways whisked me to my destinations. After college I moved to California—first Sacramento and then San Francisco and Berkeley—and then later to Seattle, Washington. The West Coast definitely felt more slow-paced, with Seattle even mellower than the Bay Area.

John and I lived for six months in Vienna, Austria, a city I love very much. There is an elegance to it as well as a precision. You could count on people being on time (or slightly early) to appointments, and the public transit system ran smoothly with delays very rare. But even with the punctual mindset, there was still a reverence for slowness. One of the things I enjoyed most there was the coffee culture, with beautiful, traditional coffee houses everywhere, and none of them served coffee to go. In Vienna, you sit down to drink your coffee slowly. It is an opportunity for pausing and savoring life.

Now we live in Galway, Ireland, a city of only eighty thousand people plus another twenty-five thousand students or so. "Irish time" is much more fluid. There isn't as much emphasis on being precise about timing.

Performances, especially evening ones, often start later than scheduled. I rarely encounter people who are overly rushed or obsessive about time or who constantly lament how busy they are. We tend to think of time as a fixed entity, the ticking seconds on the clock. But cultural values influence our experience of time.

We are exploring ways to give ourselves over to more moments of *Kairos* and reduce the experience of life's constant pressures. One of the central ways we do this is by embracing a seasonal approach to time, rather than a linear one. *Chronos* marches us forward in a straight line, so we are always running to keep up, always feeling "behind." Our language around time often reflects a keen sense of scarcity, wishing there were more hours of the day. Seasonal time is more cyclical. We revisit familiar moments with new depth and awareness. We spiral around knowing nothing is ever wasted.

The monastic tradition offers us many gifts in this regard; it is a set of practices cultivated to savor the slowness and fullness of time. We are offered practices to enter fully into the moment, so that we might discover the holy right here and now.

Praying the Hours

Our invitation is to remember who we are and why we are here. We do this, in part, by reconnecting to more ancient rhythms—not the manic, rushing clock, but the ancient rhythms of earth and body.

Many religious traditions have ways of honoring the day's unfolding by returning continuously to prayer. In the Muslim world, the call to prayer comes five times during the day. Each day is a pilgrimage through time and an opportunity to be present to the unique season each moment offers.

One of the most beautiful practices in Christian monastic tradition is the praying of the Hours. This prayer form has its roots in Jewish practice and calls us to a continuous cascade of prayer. In its most traditional form, monks would pause seven times in a day to become present again to the source and foundation of their lives. The origin of the Hours comes from the biblical encouragement in the Psalms: "Seven times a day I praise you" (Ps 119:164a).

At one time, the Book of Hours would have been carried with the same reverence with which we carry our day planners. The pages on these ancient texts were full of beauty, marvel, and wonder through word and image. There was a sense of spaciousness and time enough.

A few years ago I discovered a beautiful book—*Music of Silence: A Sacred Journey through the Hours of the Day* by David Steindl-Rast, O.S.B. (Since then Macrina Wiederkehr, O.S.B., has published her wonderful resource on praying the Hours: *Seven Sacred Pauses: Living Mindfully through the Hours of the Day.*[1]) What Br. David's book opened to me was a whole new way to experience this sacred practice. He writes, "The hours are the inner structure for living consciously and responsively through the stages of the day."[2]

The journey through the Hours is a poetic and symbolic journey through the movements of the seasons in each day. Each moment of the day has a certain kind of quality and invitation, and we are invited to make those conscious and to live our lives in response to them.

— Dawn calls us to awaken, to give thanks for a new day ahead, to shake off our slumber and what we are asleep to in life. Morning is the time when we begin work and make our commitments to the labors that sustain our lives.

— Midday is the time of the day's greatest heat and fire, but it can also be the hour when we start to lose our commitment, and so it is a good time to reignite ourselves.

— Afternoon calls us to remember the gentle fall and decline of all things as we move into evening and must embrace the beauty and poignancy of endings.

— Night in monasteries is the time of the Great Silence. The hour of darkness calls us to rest, to surrender into mystery and the unknown.

There are many ways to pray the Hours. Online there are a number of resources to aid the traditional practice of praying the psalms.[3] While the original Liturgy of the Hours has seven pauses during the day, many monastic communities have simplified this down to the four main prayer stations of morning, noon, evening, and night or Dawn, Day, Dusk, and Dark.[4] With electricity, indoor lighting can mean that the difference between these four moments is less obvious than it might once have been. And the farther you live from the equator, the more the times of dawn and dusk change throughout the year. In Ireland, during the summer the sun rises before 4 a.m. and it is not dark until almost 11 p.m., while in the heart of winter the sun rises close to 9 a.m. and sets around 4 p.m. We will be exploring seasonal rhythms in chapter 5, but know that they can have an impact on how we experience the rhythms of our days and can shift during the year.

How does the particular quality and invitation of each of these hours invite you into a deeper experience of the Holy Mystery sustaining everything and invite you to look deeper at your own beautiful heart?

How is the darkness of night similar to your own experiences of resting in unknowing? How is the breaking open of morning like your own moments of awakening to renewed purpose?

Listen for the pace of life your own body longs for. Listen for the rhythms that would support and sustain your discernment.

Praying with the Tides

> Leave me alone with God
> as much as may be.
> As the tide draws the waters close in upon the shore,
> Make me an island, set apart,
> alone with you, God, holy to you.
> Then with the turning of the tide
> prepare me to carry your presence to the busy world beyond,
> the world that rushes in on me
> till the waters come again and fold me back to you.
>
> —St. Aidan of Lindisfarne[5]

There is another daily rhythm we encounter if we live near the sea: the tide. Even if you are far from the sea, it is an amazing rhythm to contemplate and imagine. The rise and fall of the tides, which also connects us to lunar cycles (which we will explore in chapter 4), remind us again of the rise and fall of everything.

Several years ago I had the tremendous privilege of spending six months over the winter season in a small cottage by the sea. I would go to my hermitage on the Hood Canal, a fjord dividing the Kitsap and Olympic peninsulas, on the weekdays and return to our home in Seattle for the weekends. I learned so much from my time there by just being present to the tides. The beach in front of the cottage was only accessible for walking during low tide, and so the tide table became my close companion as I would time my walks to start as close to the low-tide mark as I could. On some days when, depending on the phase of the moon, the low tides weren't quite low enough to walk, I learned at what point the sandy way was open for me and when I had to release my own desires and needs.

As someone who loves to walk as a form of contemplative prayer, I found great and surprising grace in this call to pay close attention to the rhythms of the world around me, to recognize my own need to accommodate myself to the ebb and flow of the sea. We live in a world where so much of our environment is easily controlled—shopping is always accessible, we have heat for our homes to protect against the cold, and we can turn on the lights as the sun sets. So here was one place in my life where I had to surrender myself to the greater and more powerful rhythms of the world around me.

Living in Galway, I am blessed to have a view of tidal rhythms once again on a daily basis as I look over the mouth of the Corrib River where it meets the sea and witness its rise and fall. Each day I am called to consider the ways I am being invited to draw inward and outward.

All of life emerged once from the sea. If you are near a body of water of some kind—pond, lake, river, ocean—consider making time to visit its shore and spend some time in prayer and pondering. Where are the low-tide lines of your own life? Where are the primeval meeting places of earth's solidness and water's fluency? Where are you called to rest in these fertile places? How do you experience the ebb and flow of your own life? As you listen closely for your deepest call, what are the greater rhythms to which you must accommodate yourself?

Scripture Reflection from John Valters Paintner

The Laborers in the Vineyard

(Matthew 20:1-16)

For the kingdom of heaven is like a landowner who went out early in the morning to hire laborers for his vineyard. After agreeing with the laborers for the usual daily wage, he sent them into his vineyard. When he went out about nine o'clock, he saw others standing idle in the market-place; and he said to them, "You also go into the vineyard, and I will pay you whatever is right." So they went. When he went out again about noon and about three o'clock, he did the same.

—Matthew 20:1-5

In the sixth section of Matthew's gospel, Jesus leaves Galilee and goes to Judea. The crowds follow him, but Jesus continues to preach and heal them. However, not all those who come to Jesus have pure intentions.

Pharisees come to test Jesus about what the Bible has to say about divorce, but he questions their motivations and sends them away. After this the disciples try to keep people away from Jesus, even the children. But Jesus calls for the children to bless them. Next, a young rich man comes to Jesus wanting to know how to have eternal life. When Jesus tells him to sell all his possessions and give the money to the poor, the young man leaves.

Jesus turns people's expectations on their heads. In these instances, what people seem to be focusing on is not what Jesus is telling them is important. It is the same with the parable of the laborers in the vineyard.

In the parable, a farmer goes out first thing in the morning and hires day laborers to work in the fields. But by midmorning, it's clear that he needs more workers, and so he hires more. The landowner has to go back out at noon and three o'clock to hire even more workers. He even hires a last batch of laborers at five in the evening.

When the owner starts paying all the workers, he starts with those hired last and gives them the standard pay for a full day's work. Those hired first see this and start expecting a huge fee, if those who only worked an hour got so much. But when they get the usual fee, they complain. The jealousy of those hired first surprises the owner.

The reason the early-morning laborers are upset is that they had an expectation that proved to be wrong. They put a higher value on the early hour they were hired, but the equal pay all the workers received showed that the time they worked was valued as the same.

This brings us to our theme: hours. Obviously, each hour of the day is different. But they all have their own unique and equal value.

- *Morning.* Maybe you're a student or retired and a good morning is slow and leisurely. Or maybe you're a parent and/or professional and a good morning is getting everyone out of the house with as little drama as possible. Either way, how we start our day sets the tone for the rest of the day. Being intentional about how we start can make all the difference to how we end.

- *Midday.* However we start, the day can get still get away from us. Whether our day is overly full of one task after another or long and dull (perhaps even lonely), it is important to stop and pause. We all need to take a break, to catch our breath, and to look around. It's good to step back and take in the wider view—to have some perspective. We need to be cautious that we don't become burnt out or overlook the more important things in our rush to get through the day.

- *Evening.* Regardless of whether we had a good start to our day or whether we had time to pause along the way, every day ends. And the end of the day is the perfect time to reflect on it while the day's events are fresh in our minds. It is good to look back and reflect not just on what happened but also on how we handled things. This shouldn't be a time to get down on ourselves if we didn't do as well as we'd hoped, but it's an opportunity to reevaluate and refocus ourselves. As St. Benedict writes, we are to always be a beginner[6] . . . after a good night's rest.

Take some time to consider how to create a daily ritual of hours in your life: to be more intentional about every morning, to take time at midday to pause, and to make space in the evening for reflection.

Practice: Slow Awakening

What are your mornings like? Do they begin with you "alarming" yourself? Do you press the snooze button in the hope of a few more minutes of sleep? Do you feel rushed as you hurry to get to work and get on with the tasks of the day? Or do you sometimes awaken early before the dawn, unable to fall back to sleep, lying in bed wishing you could have a few more minutes of deep rest?

Are there any days during the week when you could allow yourself a slow and gentle awakening with no alarm to startle you into the day? Where you follow the natural rhythms of your body's needs?

See if you might allow yourself this gift one day each week, like a Sabbath day but without church commitments or the need to get anywhere. Allow yourself one morning when you can awaken slowly, dwelling in that liminal space between sleeping and waking. Rest there for several minutes, letting go of the need to plan the day, and just stay open to images and feelings that arise. Once you feel ready, you might journal for a few minutes, writing down anything you are aware of in this threshold place.

* Then you might prepare some coffee or tea and bring it back to bed. Spend time just sipping and gazing out the window. Listen to the birds. Let yourself daydream. Close your eyes and snooze a bit longer.

* Slow, quiet mornings such as this are some of my favorite moments. After I feed our sweet dog and let her out, my husband and I climb back into bed for snuggles, then I sip tea, read poetry and write some of my own, and record my impressions of life in my journal, the questions that linger in that open space of morning.

* How might this kind of slow awakening offer you new gifts of spaciousness and presence and a reminder of a life less pressured and harried? What does the slow awakening that would bring you the most openness look like?

Meditation: Four Daily Pauses

Your invitation is to begin to practice an awareness of the day's rhythms, or if you already pray the Hours, to deepen into your commitment to this practice. You live with some awareness of the hours of the day through the simple act of waking up each morning and going through the rituals—preparing for the day, marking the midday and dusk hours with meals of lunch and dinner, and then preparing for bed at night. However, the practice is to bring a more conscious awareness to what you are experiencing.

This practice need not take up a lot of time; it's an invitation to simply pause four times during the day. Consider putting an alarm on your phone with a gentle chime to simply call your awareness back to this moment now. Similar to the last chapter, where you were invited to pause several times a day for some long, slow, deep breaths while saying your breath prayer, now you might consider timing those pauses with these four sacred hinges of the day, in ways that work with your schedule. Your commitment is simple: a daily series of pauses. Just a few deep breaths to return to center is enough.

I offer you a meditation as a suggestion for a simple practice of pausing four times each day and facing the direction associated with that hour in the Celtic tradition (dawn is east, day is south, dusk is west, and dark is north—if you are in the southern hemisphere, reverse north and south).

We live in a world where everything is illuminated 24/7 and we are expected to be consistently productive, but eventually, we burn out from this pace of life. Here, you are invited to simply pause, connect to the rhythms of breath, notice your embodied experience in response, listen to a poem, and ponder a question. The practice can just be a five-minute pause each time, but it is a way to stay connected to the rise and fall of the day.

You are welcome to imagine yourself at each moment of dawn, day, dusk, and dark, or to enter into each part of the prayer at the corresponding time of day.

Four times each day, pause and connect to the gift and invitation of the hours of dawn, day, dusk, and dark.

Dawn

As you wake in the morning, stand and face east. Become aware of the rhythm of your breath, and allow a few moments to connect with the breath cycle. In this moment savor especially the gift of inhalation, of new life being breathed into you. Move through several cycles of breath, noticing what the moment of inhalation awakens in you this morning.

Listen to these words by the poet Rumi:

> The breeze at dawn has secrets to tell you.
> Don't go back to sleep.[7]

And let the words of Psalm 139:9–10 be on your lips:

> If I take the wings of the morning
>   and settle at the farthest limits of the sea,
> even there your hand shall lead me,
>   and your right hand shall hold me fast.

As you honor this time of awakening to a new day, pause for a moment and notice if you remember any dream fragments from the night before. Savor any images that rise up in this threshold space between sleeping and waking. What are the secrets that dawn whispers to you?

Day

In the middle of the day, perhaps before you take a break for lunch, stand and face south (north if you are in the southern hemisphere). Become aware again of the rhythm of your breath, and pause gently between your inhale and exhale, savoring this experience of being filled with oxygen and life-breath. Move through several cycles of breath just noticing what you experience in this moment of fullness.

Let the words of Psalm 55:17 be on your lips:

- Evening and morning and at noon
  I utter my complaint and moan,
  and he will hear my voice.

As you pause at midday and stand facing the south, savor this moment of full illumination. (Even if it is a cloudy or cold day, the sun is still at its peak.)

Hildegard of Bingen invites us into an intimacy with this divine fire:

- Be ablaze with enthusiasm.
  Let us be a live burning offering
  before the altar of God.[8]

How are you called to be "ablaze with enthusiasm"? What are the dreams, longings, and visions that make you feel on fire? The Desert Fathers and Mothers offer an invitation to "become fire." What might this mean for you? Where do you experience your own inner fire? What is the wild destiny the sun calls you to return to? Pause and simply be present to whatever is stirred in you in response to these questions.

Dusk

In the evening as the sun begins its descent in the sky, perhaps before your evening meal, stand and face west. Connect again to the rhythm of your breath and savor for a moment the experience of exhalation. Let each exhale be long and slow, and allow your body to release with each one. As you experience this physical letting go, notice what images or feelings stir in you.

Let these words from Psalm 113:3 be on your lips:

❧ From the rising of the sun to its setting
   the name of the LORD is to be praised.

Ponder this image from Br. David Steindl-Rast: "When evening arrives . . . people have a universal desire to find a serene place where they can put all the parts of the day together in some tranquil way. . . . At Vespers we are free to let go of the day and to luxuriate in the quiet beauty of the evening."[9]

As the sun kisses the horizon once again and you honor the descent of day into night, embrace the gift of endings. Notice what feels essential to carry with you. What are you being called to give up? What burdens get in the way of allowing your call in the world to unfold? Rest in whatever awareness wants to have some space in your imagination.

When you ponder the reality that one day your life will end, what urgency does this awareness propel you toward?

Dark

At night before bedtime, or perhaps in the middle of the night if you tend to awaken then, stand and face north (south if you are in the southern hemisphere). Become aware of the rhythm of your breath, and pause gently in the moment between your exhalation and inhalation, repeating this for several breath cycles. Sink into this moment of stillness, releasing any desire to do; allow yourself to simply be here right now.

Let the words of Psalm 46:10 be on your lips:

❧ Be still, and know that I am God!

Consider this reminder from poet Wendell Berry:

❧ To know the dark, go dark.[10]

As you honor the hour of darkness and rest, consider what it would mean for you to go into the dark without light or sight. When have you experienced the darkness as blooming and singing? What is the call of night in your life right now?

As you greet the night, welcome in the expansive mystery that night calls us to. If in your discernment you are feeling unsure, uncertain, perhaps even despairing, let night be your comfort and guide. Let the fertile darkness hold you and shape you in ways you have yet to imagine. Breathe deeply and release, resting in that emptiness, knowing that the inhalation of new ideas and vision will come again when the time is ripe. Remember that the night calls not for doing but for being.

Creative Exploration: Write a Psalm or Prayer for Each Hour

Your creative invitation is to write your own prayer for each of the hours of the day, focusing on those four thresholds or stations of dawn, midday, dusk, and nighttime. You can take your inspiration from the psalms and incorporate them into your prayers, or you might seek out contemporary poets who write about the different moments of the day. Perhaps incorporate a line from a favorite poem in each of your four prayers.

You could keep it simple and write a haiku poem for each one (haikus are composed of three lines, the first line containing five syllables, the second containing seven, and the third containing five). Or you could write a more free-form blessing. Try to keep the unique invitation that hour calls you to remember as part of your prayer. Let it serve as a reminder for the qualities of rising, fullness, falling, and emptiness and how you might reflect those qualities in your own life and daily rhythms of being.

Let your own imagination take flight, and let it be a simple prayer you recite for each of the hours as a way of grounding you in an experience of its qualities.

Closing Blessing

What are you beginning to discover as you pay attention to the unfolding of time and the rhythms of the day? What invitations are hidden inside of the hours of dawn, day, dusk, and dark? What were the moments when you paused and really touched the eternal now?

Hours

Sit under the long black branches
and await arrival of morning
light when green shoots press
forth, then pink-petaled dawn,
and finally purple weight
of a summer plum at midday
heavy with juice, afternoon
comes and I place an armful
on the table between us,
and we sit silently
by the fire savoring
sweetness well into the night.[11]

THREE

Weekly Rhythms and Sabbath Rest

> There is astounding wisdom in the traditional Jewish Sabbath, that (Sabbath) begins precisely at sundown, whether that comes at a wintry 4:30 or late on a summer evening. Sabbath is not dependent upon our readiness to stop. We do not stop when we are finished. We do not stop when we complete our phone calls, finish our project, get through this stack of messages or get out this report that is due tomorrow. We stop because it is time to stop.
>
> —Wayne Muller,
> *Sabbath: Finding Rest, Renewal, and Delight in Our Busy Lives*

The concept of Sabbath first became important to me in my twenties when I was very ill and had to take a year off from work to heal. I remember the struggles of that time, of being young and not appearing ill, of having people ask me, "What do you do?" and not knowing how to reply. Then one day I met a woman who asked me that question; I took a deep breath and started to explain that I was recovering from illness. "Oh," she said, "you're on a sabbatical." Those words opened up a whole new space and freedom within me. I suddenly recognized that what I was doing was rooted in this ancient practice and sacred tradition. It was the starting place for me to welcome this rhythm into my life.

One of my closest friends when I lived in Seattle was a rabbi, and I was deeply blessed by many invitations to her house for Friday evening dinners. I always love the rituals, prayers, and intention behind this day of rest. The Jewish practice of Sabbath has deeply informed my own. A weekly Sabbath is one of the core commitments in my own life and marriage. I would say it is perhaps one of the most essential practices and the one I fail at most regularly.

In Hebrew, the word *shabbat* (from which we get "Sabbath") means "to cease." Abraham Joshua Heschel described the Sabbath as a great cathedral or palace in time, the Jewish equivalent of sacred architecture. The meaning of Sabbath is to celebrate the holiness of time, to release the tyranny of space and the objects that demand our attention. It is a day to taste the eternal quality of life. Heschel writes that Sabbath is a "realm of time where the goal is not to have but to be, not to own but to give, not to control but to share, not to subdue but to be in accord."[1]

John and I usually set Friday night to Saturday night for our own time of weekly restoration and renewal. We describe it as a day free of work and worry, a timeless time when we can simply be present to the gifts of the day. Some weeks we struggle more with keeping this day apart than others, but I feel the difference in my week when I am able to enter into this kind of deep surrender for a day. We also try to have a technology Sabbath the entire day, releasing our constant connectedness to the outside world and the demands of emails that can be so withering to our spirits.

Sabbath calls us to remember that our purpose in life is not in doing, but in who are and were created to *be*. Work is important; it satisfies our needs to earn a living and, if we are lucky, to have creative expression, to have a place to offer our gifts in service to the world. But work can be demanding, and in the culture we live in, the drive is always to do more, produce more, and achieve more.

The invitation of entering Sabbath is to remember that we have done enough work for now and can step aside. It is an act of humility to acknowledge that the world will go on without us. We are often seduced by an artificial sense of urgency that demands an immediate response, and we don't pause to listen deeply to what is most true, to what is emerging in this moment. Sabbath offers us freedom from perpetually striving and grasping. When we embrace a Sabbath rest, we remember that life is always in process; we will never fully arrive, so we can slow down now and savor the journey.

While it may seem that this rhythm we are exploring is entirely founded in human or cultural/religious patterns, science has discovered evidence of seven-day cycles in nature through chronobiology.[2] These seven-day cycles are referred to as *circaseptan* rhythms and seem to have been present for millions of years. That this seven-day cycle appears in nature reminds us that all of creation, not just humans, needs regular time of rest and renewal. For humans, though, the rhythm of Sabbath rest helps us grow our awareness from the immediate now to the days ahead.

We expand our focus from the rhythm of the hours in each day to the rhythm of the week. I encourage you to continue with the practice of pausing four times each day. Then consider adding a time of Sabbath to your week. Experiment with allowing one day to be a time of release and renewal. There is great wisdom in designating a particular day to simply stop, despite whatever else may be going on in our lives. This is a reminder that our work is not the center of the universe, and it is an invitation to taste the eternal moment of time outside time. Walk across the threshold into Sabbath with complete awareness and attention.

Sabbath as Resistance

Theologian Walter Brueggemann has a brilliant little book titled *Sabbath as Resistance*. He describes the origins of the practice of Sabbath in the story of the Exodus in which the Israelites are freed from the "Pharaoh culture" of endless productivity and relentless labor into the "Yahweh culture" where rest is essential and we reject our slavery to perpetual anxiety. He writes:

> Into this system of hopeless weariness erupts the God of the burning bush (Exod. 3:1–6). That God heard the despairing fatigue of the slaves (2:23–25), resolved to liberate the slave company of Israel from that exploitative system (3:7–9), and recruited Moses for the human task of emancipation (3:10). The reason Miriam and the other women can sing and dance at the end of the exodus narrative is the emergence of new social reality in which the life of the Israelite economy is no

longer determined and compelled by the insatiable production quotas of Egypt and its gods (15:20–21).[3]

The God who is revealed in this story is completely unlike any they have
known before, a God committed to relationship and rest. It is worth
imagining for a moment the revolutionary power of this revelation. How
strange the Israelites must have seemed to other cultures in their radical
commitment to a day of rest each week as an act of resistance to the endless systems of anxiety. Everyone rested, no matter what gender or social
class, because God saw that as very good.

It is worth further imagining the ways that each of us is enslaved by
the current "Pharaoh culture" of perpetual overwork and exhaustion,
of busyness and relentless doing. We may have our freedom, but how
many of us choose to exercise that in favor of our own nourishment and
replenishment?

I love the image of Miriam and the other women dancing in celebration because a new story has emerged. In the scripture text one of my
favorite details is that they carried their tambourines with them in their
flight from Egypt. In the mad rush to flee death and destruction, some
of the essentials they carried with them were their musical instruments,
which allow them to revel and dance.

The Pause That Brings Meaning

✳ Sabbath ceasing [means] to cease not only from work
    itself, but also from the need to accomplish and be pro-
    ductive, from the worry and tension that accompany our
    modern criterion of efficiency, from our efforts to be in
    control of our lives as if we were God, from our pos-
    sessiveness and our enculturation, and finally, from the
    humdrum and meaninglessness that result when life is
    pursued without (God) at the center of it all.

                                                    —Marva J. Dawn,
        Keeping the Sabbath Wholly: Ceasing, Resting, Embracing, Feasting[4]

In addition to Sabbath, another vital practice in my life is yoga. Yoga offers me space to witness my own inner responses to my body's experiences, whether they be discomfort or joy. I love that most important to any yoga practice are those last few minutes when we lay in *shavasana* or corpse pose. I have often heard it said that this is the most important pose of all, because this is the place where all that has come before is integrated. In this place of rest we can bring all of our striving and work to a place of wholeness.

Sabbath serves much the same function. During Sabbath we enter into rest and stillness, release our doing, and offer ourselves a time to integrate the blessings and challenges of the week into our psyches. Just as the other poses don't hold meaning without that final pose of rest, so our work becomes an exercise in endless futility if we never offer ourselves those times to integrate—to bring in all of our experience and doing and allow ourselves just to be for a while.

Sabbath offers the gift of reminding us who we are at our deepest core so that our doing can eventually emerge from this place of being.

Many of us struggle with times of waiting, with resting in the unknown. Times of waiting can shape us into people of hope and expectation when we allow the goodness of rest to soften our alertness and our desire for something to happen now.

Sabbath is an antidote to the system of anxiety we so often find ourselves trapped in. By offering a moment to stop and step outside of our usual sense of time, Sabbath invites us into an experience of time outside of time, and in that eternal moment anxiety dissipates and slips away. We see a new reality and a new truth. We honor in the most profound way that the unfolding of events is beyond our control, and we can let go of our constant striving and manipulating of the world to make things happen. We can breathe deeply and release, just for this day, all of our concerns, emerging refreshed and renewed to face the challenges of life once again but from a different perspective.

Sabbath Moments

Consider if you might commit one day each week to the practice of Sabbath-keeping, a day to fully set aside the work of the world and embrace a time of play, rest, connection, and renewal. It doesn't have to be one of the traditional days from Jewish, Christian, or Islamic practice; just choose a day when you have the freedom to explore what Sabbath might be like for you. If you already practice a Sabbath day, consider how you might deepen your practice. Some ways to honor Sabbath are to light a candle and say a blessing to begin and end the day. Cook a beautiful meal and eat it slowly, with complete presence (see the suggested practice of slow eating later in this chapter). Take a contemplative walk or a long nap without setting the alarm. Do something playful or completely impractical. Breathe deeply.

For some of you, taking a whole day each week may be impossible due to family or work demands. I invite you to imagine how you might create Sabbath pauses during the week. Are there days when you can have a couple of hours for rest and nourishment? Perhaps you can find a two-hour window one afternoon to step away from technology and into something that feels utterly nourishing. When can you let go of the demands of daily life? No matter whether you can take an entire day or only a few hours, what is most important, I think, is to begin and end this time with intention and presence. Acknowledge that you are stepping over a threshold into a sanctuary in time.

Thomas Merton wrote about how overwork can be a form of violence to ourselves. One of my favorite quotes is in *Conjectures of a Guilty Bystander*. Writing to peace activists and those in ministry and service, he says that "the rush and pressure of modern life are a form, perhaps the most common form, of its innate violence."[5] Sabbath is an antidote to this violence. Consider Sabbath as a time when you vow not to harm anyone or anything. Move through the day with utter presence to the life force within you and the world around you. Take a contemplative walk and allow each step to gently kiss the earth. Remember that you are a guest, and receive the earth's hospitality.

Saying no is as important as saying yes. Again and again in our lives we are called upon to meet the needs of others, offered opportunities, and presented with possibilities. Saying no comes from a deeply centered place where we recognize that our yes only has meaning in the context of what we do not allow to take up our time. We say no to be fully free to say yes.

How might your practice of Sabbath be an act of cultivating peace and nonviolence? What are the places in your life where you are experiencing a lack of freedom? How might the practice of saying no help to break open new possibilities?

Scripture Reflection from John Valters Paintner

Bricks without Straw

(Exodus 5:1-23)

Afterward Moses and Aaron went to Pharaoh and said, "Thus says the LORD, the God of Israel, 'Let my people go, so that they may celebrate a festival to me in the wilderness.'" But Pharaoh said, "Who is the LORD, that I should heed him and let Israel go? I do not know the LORD, and I will not let Israel go." . . .

Then Moses turned again to the LORD and said, "O LORD, why have you mistreated this people? Why did you ever send me? Since I first came to Pharaoh to speak in your name, he has mistreated this people, and you have done nothing at all to deliver your people."

—Exodus 5:1-2, 22-23

Moses's story starts with his birth, when his mother and sister save him from execution by floating him down the river in a basket. The Pharaoh's daughter adopted Moses, and Moses grows up in the Pharaoh's palace. But as a young man, Moses flees Egypt after he kills an Egyptian he had witnessed beating an Israelite. (Unlike most film adaptations of this story, scripture indicates that Moses grew up knowing he was an Israelite by birth.)

Moses begins a new life, becoming a shepherd and starting a family. He has no plans ever to return to Egypt, when God speaks to him through a burning bush, calling Moses to lead the Israelites out of Egypt. Moses is very reluctant to heed God's call, but eventually he relents and reunites with his brother Aaron.

Chapter 5 begins when Moses and Aaron first confront the Pharaoh and ask permission to take the Israelites into the desert to worship Yahweh, one of the first mentions of the Sabbath. Moses is uniquely qualified for this task. Not only has he been blessed by God with many gifts but also he grew up in the royal palace. It's unclear from the text if Moses knows this current Pharaoh or if the Pharaoh recognizes Moses after so long an absence, but Moses has intimate working knowledge of Egyptian palace politics. Unfortunately, other than getting an audience with the Pharaoh, this knowledge doesn't help Moses's cause.

The Pharaoh's initial response ("Who is this 'LORD' person and why should I listen to him?") is understandable from his perspective. This request from representatives of his slaves comes out of the blue for him. It gets worse when the Pharaoh realizes that Moses and Aaron want to take his workforce on a three-day journey into the desert to worship a god he's never heard of. He refuses, and when Moses tries to push the issue, the Pharaoh falsely accuses the Israelites of being lazy and just wanting to get out of work. As punishment (for the crime of asking for a few days off), the Pharaoh takes away some of the building materials he had been supplying the Israelites with and yet demands the same productivity.

The Pharaoh's taskmasters and supervisors do as instructed, and the plight of the Israelites—who were so hopeful with the arrival of Moses and the promise of Yahweh's help—becomes much worse. Not only must the Israelites keep up their daily production quota of bricks but also they must now do so while collecting all the needed materials themselves. When they fall behind, the beatings begin. But rather than blame Pharaoh for his added cruelty, the Israelites berate Moses for starting the trouble. The chapter ends with Moses asking the Lord why he was sent on such a task, and he blames God for the further mistreatment of the Israelites.

But God is not responsible for the mistreatment, nor are the task-masters and supervisors, even though they participate in the Pharaoh's unjust orders. The decision to increase the Israelites' work falls solely at the feet of the Pharaoh. The cause of their problems is the Pharaoh's pride, which will become a central figure as this story unfolds. But why is the Pharaoh so put out by a simple request? Why doesn't he just say no and move on? Why the extra work as punishment? What is it that has him so upset?

Even though the Pharaoh was seen as part of the pantheon of Egyptian gods, he doesn't seem at all concerned about his foreign slaves worshiping their foreign God, as long as the number of bricks doesn't decrease. It's odd that he's most upset about a reduction in productivity.

This is what sets up the underlying difference between the Israelites and the Egyptians. It is not that one is monotheistic and one is not (although *monotheistic* means something different to the Israelites during the time of the Exodus than to later generations of Israelites, and the ten plagues can be interpreted as Yahweh defeating the Egyptian gods to free the Chosen People from bondage). It's not even so much that one is powerful and one is powerless (although that is an important, recurring theme throughout the Bible—God favors the poor and oppressed). The significant difference here, which the Pharaoh sets up with his fake concern about the false claim of Israelite laziness, is that one is only concerned about productivity and the other is concerned with worship. One of these two parties is very caught up in worldly desires, while the other is trying to focus on more spiritual matters.

Pharaoh is the only one who sets up a false dichotomy: work versus not-work. Moses, on behalf of Yahweh, is asking that the people be able to set aside some time for spiritual matters while not neglecting their earthly responsibilities. Pharaoh is so concerned with productivity that he won't give in to any demands for time off from his slave labor. Later in this story, he even demands more productivity when Moses and Aaron return with their request for time off to worship. It is only after Pharaoh proves unreasonable to any com- promise that the Israelites, through Yahweh's help, flee his slavery completely.

It is not that work, in and of itself, is bad. Work, for the right rea- sons and in right balance, can be very good. It can bring meaning and joy. It can be an act of love, providing for the needs of loved ones. But all work and no worship makes for an empty soul.

And so this work/worship debate comes down to balance, a balance achieved by a rhythm. And the rhythm laid out, repeated throughout Hebrew and Christian scripture, is that of a weekly Sab- bath. A six-to-one ratio may seem a bit unbalanced toward work, but when the focus of the weekly work is toward the weekend Sabbath, right balance is achieved.

The traditional nine-to-five, Monday-through-Friday workweek has been turned on its head of late. Whether one is a student or retired, traditionally employed or self-employed in the new gig econ- omy, or working in a pastoral setting where Sabbath is the busiest day of one's week, we all need to find our own path, our own balance. And that can look very different even for people in similar external situations because of everyone's unique internal spiritual life.

How do you balance work and worship? Where do you plant your flag of Sabbath and orientate everything else around it?

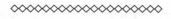

Practice: Slow Eating

Sadly we live in a fast-food culture focused more on speed and conve- nience than on the pleasures of eating. One of the things we love to do as part of our Sabbath day is to make a home-cooked dinner and invite a friend or two to share it with us. In general, we really enjoy cooking during the week, but Sabbath dinner takes on a special significance. This meal is at a threshold moment as we mark our entrance into the day of rest, and when we get to share the meal with friends, it becomes an act of communion and celebration.

There is great wisdom in the way the Jewish day begins the evening before, rather than at midnight. Sabbath doesn't start in the middle of the night when we are asleep; it begins as the sun dips below the horizon and the sky grows dark. In the midst of that growing darkness our invitation is to light candles, say blessings, and savor a meal together slowly.

The Latin root of the word "savor" is *saporem*, which is connected to *sapientiae*, the word for "wisdom." Savoring can only be done slowly; it is inherently an activity that cannot be rushed, for if it were rushed, it would no longer be savoring. Savoring also brings us wisdom. Wisdom emerges not from rushing through life to find answers but from a long, slow reflection on the life questions that echo within our hearts.

Sabbath allows us time to savor our meal and the company we keep. We don't have to prepare anything fancy; even a beautiful bowl of berries or a plate of simply cooked vegetables can be enough. But when it's done with love and reverence, we enter into a space where everything feels generous and abundant. When we slow down, we can bring our senses alive and attune ourselves to not only the taste but also the sight (colors), smell (aroma and fragrance), feel (textures on the tongue), and sound (conversation and perhaps music) of the meal. We feel much more nourished when we can savor a meal and allow it to fill us in ways that our rushed moments during the rest of the week never can.

Meditation: Reflecting on the Week with the Examen Prayer

This guided meditation is an adaptation of the Examen prayer developed by St. Ignatius of Loyola as a reflection on the life-giving and life-draining moments of your week, a central practice for discernment. In this adaptation of the meditation, we will be reflecting on moments in our week that felt restful and those that felt busy and distracted.

In this experience, I will be inviting you to bring your body into the prayer through gentle arm stretches in different directions. You are also welcome to engage the prayer without the movement or to simply imagine yourself stretching.

The Examen prayer is a simple but profound way of tending to interior movements over time. It can be done on a daily basis for personal prayer, but my favorite way to practice it is as part of my Sabbath ritual. Reflecting on my week, I listen for the experiences that felt full of grace and those that were challenging. Then John and I share with each other what emerged in prayer. It is a beautiful way to share the week's journey in a sacred way.

Preparation

You may do this prayer sitting, standing, or entirely in your imagination. Begin by moving your attention inward. Center yourself by getting in touch with your body and breath. Become aware of the presence of God within the earth of your heart. Listen deeply to your body and its messages.

Reaching Both Arms Down

Become aware of your connection to the earth and its support beneath you. What do you need to ground you and bring your awareness to the present moment? What concerns keep you from being fully here in this Sabbath time? Can you allow your exhale to gently release these for this time of prayer? What is awakening beneath the ground of your being?

Reaching Back behind You with Right Arm

Looking back on this last week, when did you feel most at ease? Most rested and renewed? Most alive and free of pressure and anxiety? Where did you feel most filled with love? Hope? Notice which moment or experience arises, and enter into it again. Take a few moments to experience this in your body. How does revisiting this moment feel for you? Is there anyone you want to thank for this memory? Spend a few moments dwelling in gratitude. Bring your right arm back along your side.

Reaching Back behind You with Left Arm

Looking back at this past week, when did you feel the most anxious or distracted? Most exhausted or overwhelmed by life's burdens? Where did you feel most restless? The least hopeful? Notice which moment or experience arises, and enter into it again. How does revisiting this moment feel for you in your body? Take a few moments to experience this. Is there anyone you want to offer forgiveness for this experience (including yourself)? Spend a few moments seeing if you are moved to extend forgiveness. Bring your left arm back along your side.

Reaching Both Arms Forward

Holding a heart of gratitude and forgiveness, how do you want to move forward into this Sabbath day? What are your hopes? How are you being invited to follow the Spirit now? What is your intention and deep heart's desire for this time ahead? How do you nurture the new seeds of life stirring within you?

Reaching Both Arms Upward

What guidance do you need to support you in your Sabbath practice? What do you want to ask for to help you move more fully into your hopes for the day? How might you call on God for this guidance?

Reaching Inward

Bringing your hands to prayer position or leaving them open in a receiving posture, what new things do you notice now stirring within you? What is awakening within you? What desires and insights invite further reflection? Allow a few minutes to simply rest in this posture, breathing and receiving, without needing to do anything.

Following the meditation, you might want to take a few minutes to journal about anything you noticed.

Creative Exploration: Contemplative Photography

You are invited into the practice of contemplative photography, which is a practice of going out into the world with camera in hand to pay attention and receive the gifts offered. It is not about making something happen or trying to have a particular kind of experience.

Visio divina (sacred seeing) is a way of seeing the world with the eyes of the heart, which is the place of receptivity and openness, rather than with the mind, which is often the place of grasping and planning. Rather than taking or capturing photos, we are receiving images as gifts. It is an adaptation of the ancient practice of *lectio divina* (sacred reading).

Your sole focus is on being present to each moment's invitation as it unfolds rather than setting out with a particular goal. There is nowhere to get to. You begin by breathing deeply and centering yourself, bringing your awareness down to your heart center. Then go on a contemplative walk, open to receiving images of rest. What does rest look like for you? As you consider this question, see where your attention is drawn, keeping an open awareness to what you encounter along the way.

Settling and Shimmering

Breathe deeply. Move your awareness down to your heart center. Settle into this moment. Release any thoughts or expectations. See if you can keep a soft gaze, which is diffuse and open, as opposed to a hard stare when you are looking for something.

As you begin walking, let your experience itself be restful; there is nothing you have to do. Pay attention to things around you that shimmer, which means something that calls for your attention and invites you to spend some time with it. It might be a natural object such as a tree or branch; it might be a sign in a shop window that catches your attention or the way light is flooding the street. Stay open to all possibilities for how the world might speak to your heart about what rest looks like.

Savoring and Stirring

Stay with what shimmers, and allow it to unfold in your heart, savoring your experience.

Make space within for images, feelings, and memories to stir. How does your body respond? What are you noticing happening inside in response to this experience?

Summoning and Serving

Slowly shift your awareness to a sense of invitation or summoning that rises up from your prayer. How does the prayer stirring in you meet you in this particular moment of your life? How might you be called into a new awareness or kind of service through this experience? What longing does this image of rest stir in your heart?

You might explore with your camera how gazing at this shimmering moment through the lens supports you in seeing it more deeply. If you notice yourself grasping, put the camera down. But if the lens helps you to see this moment from different perspectives and deepen into it, the camera can be a great gift.

Slowing and Stilling

Once your walk feels complete, return home and release all of the words and images and slow down even more deeply. Allow yourself some time for silence and stillness. Breathe gratitude in and out. Simply notice your experience. Spend some time journaling what you noticed and discovered.

Closing Blessing

Allow some time to ponder your own patterns of overwork and striving. Reflect on times of forced rest such as illness, and ponder your response to the experience. Were you able to release into it? Are there worries and tensions that need surrendering? Are there ways that you use work to pretend you are fully in control of your life?

What are the things you need to unplug from to truly experience Sabbath freedom?

When you allow yourself to fully enter into the gift of Sabbath rest, what do you notice about your mind, heart, and body? What is your felt experience of deep peace?

Sabbath

Even as the subway car hurtles
into the tunnel and calendars heave
under growing weight of entries,
even under the familiar lament
for more hours to do

a bell rings somewhere
and a man lays down
his hammer, as if to say
the world can build without me,
a woman sets down
her pen as if to say,
the world will carry on
without my words.

The project left undone,
dust on the shelves,
dishes crusted with morning
egg, the vase of drooping
flowers, and so much work
still to complete,

I journey across the long field
where trees cling to the edges
free to not do anything but
stand their ground,
where buttercups
and bluebells sway

and in this taste of paradise
where rest becomes luminous
and play a prayer of gratitude,
even the stones sing

of a different time,
where burden is lifted
and eternity endures.[6]

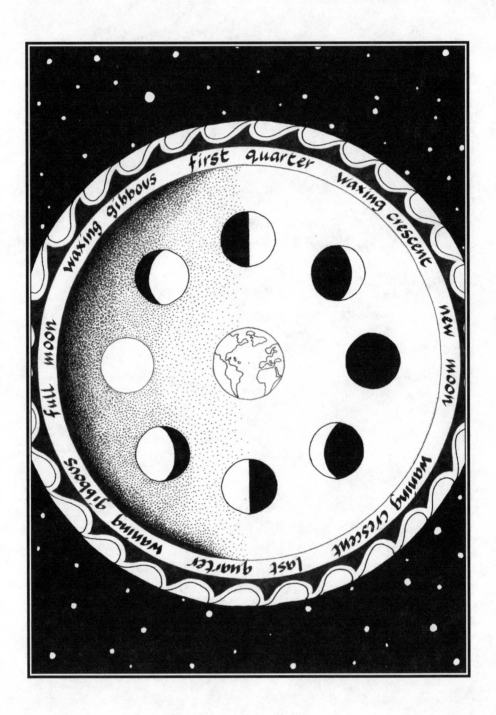

FOUR

Waxing and Waning Lunar Cycles

Praised be You, my Lord, through Sister Moon and the stars,
In the heavens you have made them bright, precious and fair.
—St. Francis of Assisi, "Canticle of Creation"

St. Francis was a true nature mystic; he considered all of creation as our kin, including the celestial bodies of Brother Sun and Sister Moon. We explored in the last chapter what a Sabbath rhythm might look like in our week with times of both preparation and savoring. We continue this expansion outward in time by looking at the cycles of the moon and how we might bring an awareness of the waxing and waning each month into our lives and prayer. We live in a time when we can easily ignore the phases of the moon. We spend our nights indoors with artificial illumination and lose our connection to this primal rhythm.

Both the Jewish and Islamic calendars are lunar calendars, and feasts are calculated according to the moon's rhythms. In Judaism each new month begins at the new moon, whereas our Gregorian calendar is based on the solar year, and so the months are roughly an artificial construct to divide the year into equal parts.

Much of the Christian calendar is based on the Gregorian calendar, but we do find some traces of the lunar calendar in the Christian feast of Easter, which is on the first Sunday after the first full moon after the vernal equinox. It is calculated on a combination of both lunar and solar rhythms. We also see the influence of the lunar calendar in Christianity in how moon phases are referred to often in the scriptures.

I find great wisdom in how the Jewish month begins with the new moon, the place of darkness and stillness from which life emerges. This same wisdom is seen in how in Jewish practice the day begins the night before, and in Christian tradition our feasts also begin with a vigil on the evening prior. This black, fertile expanse is the sacred container for what is to come. Before we anticipate the blossoming, we must sink deeply into the gift of rest that beckons from the night. In the Celtic calendar, the year begins at Samhain, November 1, the Feast of All Saints, followed by the Feast of All Souls. Similarly, the Christian liturgical calendar begins anew each Advent with the descent into darkness in the northern hemisphere.

Moon time is also closely connected to a woman's menstrual cycle, and when women lived in close community with one another, their cycles aligned around the new moon and they could anticipate their bodies' changes by the way the moon was changing in the sky. As such the moon has often been considered feminine and is tied to the ancient understanding of the phases of a woman's life as maiden, mother, and crone. The moon also affects the rise and fall of the tides, which we explored in our chapter on the rhythms of the day.

The moon has much wisdom to offer us with her witness to the necessity of both waxing and waning, both brilliant fullness and utter darkness. At every turn it seems that nature calls us to embrace both expansion and contraction as necessary to the very way we were created.

The moon was significant to our ancestors in faith in many ways. The night sky was once an important navigational tool; in the Christian scriptures we read about the wise men who followed the star to where Jesus lay (see Mt 2:2). In the Hebrew Scriptures Abraham was told by God that his descendants would number the stars (see Gn 15:5). The heavens are God's "handiwork" (Ps 19:1; cf. 8:3). God has all the stars numbered and named (see Ps 147:4). We might imagine how vast the night sky seemed to ancient peoples, especially during long, winter nights, and how God's promise to Abraham was rooted in a sense of the immensity of the number of celestial bodies. As we take time to reconnect with the luminaries in the heavens, especially the moon, we can reconnect to this sense of awe that filled the hearts of our ancestors.

If you don't already, I invite you to begin to keep track of the lunar cycles, making note of the full and new moons on your calendar so you become aware of the rhythms of waxing and waning in the night sky. Consider making time at the next full moon to be outside and moon-gaze.

I have heard the moon referred to as Grandmother Moon because of her ancient wisdom. What name would you like to offer to the moon? As you listen for how your life is unfolding, what is the energy that you need to call upon to support you as you move forward?

Moon Cycles

> Raise a song, sound the tambourine,
> 　　the sweet lyre with the harp.
> Blow the trumpet at the new moon,
> 　　at the full moon, on our festal day.

—Psalm 81:2–3

> There will be signs in the sun, the moon, and the stars.

—Luke 21:25

> A great portent appeared in heaven: a woman clothed with the sun, with the moon under her feet, and on her head a crown of twelve stars.

—Revelation 12:1

Astrology is an ancient way of reading the movement of the sky as symbolic for the movement of our lives. Just as the sun moves through various astrological signs, so does the moon. It cycles through all twelve signs within the space of a month's time. At the new moon it is in the same sign as the sun; and at the full moon, when the moon is opposite the sun in the sky, it is in the opposite sign as the sun. You often find the zodiac, various astrological symbols, and constellation charts adorning many medieval churches.

For the last several years I have been tracking the new and full moons in my own life, taking time on these days to reflect. The new moon is

considered to be a threshold to new beginnings, the time of resting in
the emptiness the way we did with the breath. At this phase of darkness
we can plant seeds for what will emerge. At the full moon we celebrate
what has come into full ripeness and illumination. One way I have been
able to celebrate the full moon this past summer is with a local perfor-
mance artist who began leading monthly sea-swim rituals for women
on the full moon. During these rituals, we gather by the sea, begin with
a meditation, then anoint ourselves with oil before diving into the sea
together for a brisk dip. When we emerge, we have tea together and time
to chat. It is a really beautiful way of honoring this primal cycle.

The moon offers us another window into sacred time, marking the
turning of the earth and inviting us into a meditation on the times for
waxing, for fullness, for waning, and for darkness. The time of waxing is
akin to the inhale and to the dawn, the full moon parallels the moment
of fullness in the breath and the hour of midday, the waning moon car-
ries a similar energy to the exhale and the time of dusk, and the new
moon or dark moon is similar to the moment of emptiness in the breath
and the hour of midnight. When we observe her rhythms month after
month, we can grow in trust of her regular emergence from the darkness. This, perhaps, allows us to sink more easily into the letting go. We
can learn to trust the times of waning and rest as part of a larger cycle
of time.

Honoring the cycles of the moon means cultivating a familiarity with,
and even a love of, the darkness. Just as each breath begins and ends in
emptiness, just as each day emerges from the nighttime, the moon wid-
ens and grows smaller again until she disappears. We live in a culture
of productivity, where we value the energy of dawn and midday much
more than dusk and night. We want to be always waxing or full, and we
often resist the waning and the emptiness. But what if we were to view
those dark hours and barren seasons as integral to our wholeness? What
if the exhaustion we chronically feel is a sign that we need the gift of deep
rest and to follow the moon's guidance? How might our own faith be cultivated by tending these cycles, so that we grow in trust in both the waxing and the waning and know that neither is the end of the story?

How might you make the lunar cycles a more conscious and intentional part of your spiritual practice? Even if you live someplace, as I do,

where the sky is often cloudy or where there is too much light pollution to easily see the moon, how might imagining the moon's presence in the sky and becoming aware of the direction of her movement deepen your own connection to your internal rhythms?

Dreams of the Heart

In his book *Drawing Closer to Nature*, Peter London writes:

> We too are remnants of that First Fire that ever since lights the heavens as well as the tiny fires that warm our brief lives. Our planet remembers this original heat deep within its core, as we do in our fashion. . . . The setting of our life's journey takes places upon a stage in which we spend half our allotted time in yellow light from a ball of Fire, the other half in pale blue light from a mirror-ball. We are diurnal creatures formed with all the rest of the biota upon a diurnal planet. The two lights provide us with different-appearing worlds, which in turn form our two different minds; the one that reasons and the one that dreams.[1]

The moon rules over the night. We see her best when the sky is dark and we are alert to her position in the sky, which requires that we pay attention and open ourselves to the call of the dark. Night is also the time for dreams, which offer us wisdom for our times of discernment. The moon reigns over dreamtime.

Dream-tending is one of my primary spiritual practices. I deeply believe that our dreams are gifts from a divine Source of wisdom that is far greater than our waking consciousness. I like to think of dreams as the moon singing to us of our heart's deep desires as we sleep. Dreams are deeply honored in both Hebrew and Christian scriptures as modes of revelation and guidance, as well as playing a significant role in Celtic Christian practice. There are many stories of biblical figures and Irish saints receiving wisdom and direction in their dreams such as Jacob, Joseph in both the Old and New Testaments, and Saints Ciaran and Gobnait to name a few.

Our dreams are not bound by the cognitive restrictions of our waking life—they speak in a different language from our usual linear and rational thinking, in the language of poetry and image and symbol. They let us know how we really feel and think, not the way we pretend to think and feel, and so help us to live more deeply from our authentic selves. They also reveal what our conscious mind doesn't already know, moving us toward an awareness of deeper truths not always apparent in our conscious, waking state. A prominent dream worker, Jeremy Taylor, said that all dreams come in the service of health and wholeness and that "bad dreams" are usually those that are really trying to grab our attention.

Dreams are always inviting me to a bigger reality than the one I live in. They are a deep source of wisdom for our spiritual lives. I love that when we go to sleep and are in a state of deep surrender, we can't help but be creative, creating stories and images that invite us to live a bigger life.

We don't live in a culture that honors dream wisdom. With our societal emphasis on productivity and speed, taking time to listen to dreams and allow them to unfold can seem like a waste of time. We value facts and figures over the mercurial and unknown. Yet, there are many cultures, especially indigenous ones, that revere dreams and what they have to offer. Honoring dreams and the unconscious takes deliberate nurture and attention. I find that awareness of dreams is usually in response to our attitudes toward them. The more we honor them and make space for them, the more likely we are to remember them consistently and learn from their wisdom.

Dreams usually have multiple meanings and layers of significance. The different dream symbols usually represent different elements of ourselves, so a dream about a friend or spouse may not be about them so much as what their qualities represent in our own self. It is wise to approach dreams with humility and unknowing and not co-opt the dream messages for our own agendas.

Dreams can be especially helpful to pay attention to during times of discernment and transition. Carl Jung said that our primary language is image, and so the newness that is being born in us during times of change is first articulated in symbol and image. Only later do we bring language to express it.

I find being part of a dream group to be enormously helpful in the ongoing work of dream-tending. Dreams often reveal our blind spots, so other people can notice things we don't and help us keep our agendas from influencing our understanding of our dreams. Bring your dream to a spiritual director or cherished friend, and ask if they can help you to see things that have been hidden to you. Remember that while a friend's perspective is helpful, only you as the dreamer can say with any certainty what meaning your dream may have. That meaning usually comes in the form of a wordless "aha!" moment of recognition. Allow the images and meanings of the dream to emerge slowly over time like the moon from her darkness.

What if we lived dream-centered lives and, when we woke up in the morning, we could sit down to a leisurely breakfast with our loved ones and share our dreams from the previous night? What if our churches became places of really honoring dreams? What might be waiting to break through by the simple act of giving your dreams a privileged place in your waking consciousness? How might dreams illuminate your path?

Scripture Reflection from John Valters Paintner

The Beginning of Jesus' Passion and the Signs of the End Times

(Luke 19:28–21:28)

There will be signs in the sun, the moon, and the stars, and on the earth distress among nations confused by the roaring of the sea and the waves. People will faint from fear and foreboding of what is coming upon the world, for the powers of the heavens will be shaken. Then they will

see "the Son of Man coming in a cloud" with power and
great glory. Now when these things begin to take place,
stand up and raise your heads, because your redemption
is drawing near.

—Luke 21:25-28

This passage from Luke comes toward the end of his gospel in a section that begins with Jesus entering Jerusalem in glory. Jesus sends
two disciples ahead of him to procure a colt for him to ride into the
city in order to fulfill a prophecy about the Messiah. Jesus would
have been aware of this passage, as would those who witnessed him
on the colt. He is making a deliberate statement. While the Romans
were oblivious to the symbolism of the colt, his fellow Jews understood what he was doing and why. Some Pharisees objected, but
when the crowds saw Jesus on the colt, they greeted him with shouts
of praise.

Despite the jubilant reception of the masses, Jesus weeps over
the city. He is not concerned about his own fate; he is troubled by the
trials and tribulations that were in store for the inhabitants of Jerusalem in the coming years.

Next, Jesus turns his attention to the Temple, where he drives
out those taking financial advantage of those wishing to make sac-
rifices. Jesus' disruption of "business as usual" at the Temple led to
the chief priests and scribes questioning his authority to preach. But
Jesus refuses to play into their trap and continues to communicate
his message. He tells the parable of the wicked tenants, in which a
man plants a vineyard and leaves it in the care of tenants. When the
harvest comes and the man sends a servant to collect his share, the
tenants beat the servant and send him away. The man sends a second and a third servant, both of whom are similarly mistreated by
the tenants. Finally the owner of the vineyard sends his son, figuring
that the tenants would not dare mistreat him. But the tenants, hoping
to inherit the vineyard themselves, kill the man's son. Jesus ends the
parable by asking what should become of the tenants. It is then that

the chief priests and scribes know that Jesus is talking about them, and so they flee.

They then send spies to try to trap Jesus. These dishonest servants of the chief priests and scribes ask Jesus if they should pay taxes to the Romans, hoping any answer would either anger the Jewish crowds or get him in trouble with the Romans. But Jesus silences them by saying, "Give to the emperor the things that are the emperor's, and to God the things that are God's" (Lk 20:25).

Next some Sadducees ask Jesus a question about heaven with a tragic story about a widow who had had several husbands who all died. Jesus sees through their hypothetical question and speaks of the need to think beyond the concerns of the present age to the age of resurrection. Even some of the scribes are impressed by Jesus' answer and dare not question him further. Jesus then turns the tables on them by asking them a question about who is greater: King David or the Messiah, the one who was or the One who is to come?

Jesus next goes to his disciples and warns them not to be like the scribes who care most about appearance. He gives the example of the widow who gave two coins as a true role model, for even though she did not give much, what she did give was most of what she had. This was unlike the scribes who gave much but who had so much more that they kept for themselves.

He goes on to foretell of the destruction of the Temple. Jesus tells the people that it will be torn down, not one stone left on another. When they ask him when this will happen, Jesus warns them against false messiahs and of the signs to come. He warns them of the dark days ahead and tells them to be prepared for persecution, but he will be with them and help them endure.

So with all these teachings, as part of his Passion, Jesus foretells the coming end times. The people, rightfully concerned, ask for signs to know when all this will come to be. Jesus gives them many signs to look out for, most of them unfortunately common things such as war and persecution, and warns them of false prophets out to deceive them. But among all the anxiety and confusion is a clear message: look to the heavens. Jesus tells the people to look to the heavens, the sun and moon and stars, for signs of the time to come. When they see the powers of the heavens, they will know the time of their redemption is drawing near.

In California, where I grew up, there wasn't much of a change from one season to the next. The dark, shorter evenings of winter were marked by daylight savings time just before Halloween. Summer was marked by the end of the school year. Fall and spring were barely noticed. I never had seasonal clothes. There was never a time of putting away lighter-weight garments to make room in the closet for heavy winter coats. It just wasn't a thing. And I didn't even live anywhere near the equator.

But one thing that was noticeable, in part because of the almost-constant clear skies, was the moon. There weren't a lot of stars visible in the suburbs with its plethora of streetlights. But one could keep track of the phases of the moon easily enough, if one was to pay attention and look up.

Looking up at the moon is one of the few universal experiences— and perhaps this is why Jesus told us that signs of the end times would be in the moon and other heavenly bodies. The moon transcends culture and geography. We can all see it. There's even a practice of telling a loved one far away to look up at the moon at night and be comforted by the fact that the two of you are looking up at the same moon.

The moon isn't always visible, because of daylight or cloud cover or the monthly new moon. But it is still there. The rising and setting of the moon, along with its particular phases, can be found in everything from old-time almanacs to newfangled weather apps.

While most people are only interested in the full or new moon, there are quarter, crescent, and gibbous moons, and all the time the moon is waxing or waning. And in many ways, I prefer the in-between phases of the moon. I like that it's not always easy to tell how close or far the moon is from one of the four main phases (new, first quarter, and full). I don't follow the moon's progress as closely as Christine, so often when I look up at the night sky, I am not sure if it's just past or about to be one of those four.

They look the same to my untrained eye. But I think there's a life lesson there: If all we get is a glimpse of someone, we can't really know what trajectory they are on. We tend to see isolated behavior by others and assume it is how they habitually are, while excusing our own inconsistencies by assuming that we are just one thing. The crowds greeting Jesus on the colt entering Jerusalem saw him as the great judge sent to free them from Roman occupation. The chief priests who saw Jesus overturn the money changers' tables at the Temple saw a threat to their power. Neither saw all sides of Jesus, and so they had a distorted view of who he was and how such seemingly opposite actions were part of a more coherent narrative. We must be careful not to have one image of someone else and think that is the totality of who they are, were, and ever will be. We also need to be both honest about the many sides of who we are (not just always light or dark, but always somewhere along the spectrum in between) and kind to ourselves through our waning times (because, like the moon, we will soon be waxing again). The gentle, slow waxing and waning are phases we all experience.

What signs help comfort you in times of trouble? Metaphorically, what phase are you in? Are you waxing or waning?

Practice: Slow Dreaming

Keep a notebook and pen by your bed so that you can signal to your unconscious the importance of dreams for you and then write your dream down upon waking. The further you move into waking consciousness, the further the dream will slip away. As you go to bed at night, open your heart to receive the gift of a dream. Consider creating a nighttime ritual to welcome the gift of dreams into your life. Turn off your electronic devices an hour before bed, prepare some herbal tea, take a bath (or even just a foot bath), place a notebook and pen by your bed, and ask for a dream.

When you awaken from a dream, try to stay still for a few moments and reinhabit the dream space, noticing how you are feeling, what is happening, and who is there. I often wake from a dream and take a few minutes to close my eyes and walk around the dream landscape, seeing what I can hold onto to carry into waking.

After you have spent a few moments reinhabiting the dream space, write the date and a description of the dream recorded in present tense. Writing in past tense has the effect of putting distance between you and the dream. Give a title to your dream, something to help you remember it when you flip through your dream journal. In the description include the setting, people, animals, objects, actions/plot, and feelings.

As you make a practice of writing down your dreams, I recommend you include not only the date but also the moon phase in your journal. You might begin to notice a pattern of dreams that reflect the rhythm of waxing and waning.

Then call on the moon to support your dream life. Consider engaging in an adaptation of the ancient practice of *lectio divina*. Let the moon be your sacred text. Allow some time to sink into stillness, ground your body, and connect with your breath. As you gaze upon the moon, become present to any images or words it stirs in you. What is shimmering for you as you behold her presence? Let those rise up and then expand your imagination, paying attention to feelings or memories that unfold for you. Simply make space for the images that come. After some time spent in open receiving, consider: What is the invitation for you from this time of prayer? From what you have seen and experienced, is there a sense of being called forward into a particular action or awareness? Close with a few moments of simply being, resting into silence.

Meditation: Working with a Dream

Upon waking from a dream, write it down as closely as you can to the experience, and then spend some time reflecting with the questions that follow. I recommend doing this from a meditative and open state of awareness, so spend a few moments centering and opening yourself to the gift of receiving any insights that may arise. We approach dreams from the intuitive part of ourselves, as they speak not in linear and logical language but in symbols, feeling, and experience. These questions will help you explore those symbols, feelings, and experiences.

What are the feelings you are most aware of in the dream? Have you felt this way in your past or current waking life?

Describe the setting of the dream. Does it remind you of any place in waking life? What are your associations with this setting or place? For instance, if there was a house in the dream, how would you define a house to someone who didn't know what that was? Notice the language used in these explanations. How does it feel to be in this setting?

What are the other dream symbols such as persons, animals, or objects? What are your associations with each person, animal, or object? For instance, if someone you know appears in the dream, describe your relationship to this person and how you would express who they are. Again, notice the language used in these explanations. Do they remind you of any part of yourself? Is there a time in your life when you embody these qualities?

Describe the major action in this dream. Does it remind you of any situation in your waking life?

Consider why this particular dream came to you at this particular time. What is happening in the context of your life that may add insight into the dream's meaning?

Creative Exploration: The Art of Dreaming

The arts can be especially helpful in working with a dream, as they use the same language of symbols, feelings, and experiences for expression. There are many ways you can bring the arts into service to help you break a dream open.

You might begin by writing your dream down using colored pens or pencils. Use a different color for each word, and let your color choice be intuitive. Draw symbols for the nouns and verbs alongside the words you use so that the expression of the dream becomes multidimensional.

Another way to work with dream images is through movement. Spend some time embodying one of the dream energies or characters. It could be a person, an animal, or even a vehicle or an object—whatever part of the dream seems to have the most energy for you. Allow your movement to unfold. What does it feel like to move through the world as this being?

Allow a gesture to be formed out of the movements. Is there a shape or gesture that expresses the heart of this dream symbol for you? You can experiment with several of the dream symbols in this way, allowing each to settle into a shape or gesture, and then at the end create a dance that moves through these various shapes and see how the journey is unfolding within you through movement. The dream might even continue on from where it ended in your sleep to offer you new direction or insight.

After some time spent with drawing and movement, allow some moments for silence in order to integrate and feel how the dream has shifted within you. Then take some time to journal. Resist the urge to make the dream mean something right away. It often takes time to coax out the meaning for us. Pay attention to synchronicities in your life as well, moments when the dream symbols may appear in other contexts of your daily activity.

Closing Blessing

Consider how you might cultivate your awareness and honoring of these rhythms over the coming months. Perhaps it's just by marking the moon phases in your calendar at the four turning points of new moon, first quarter (waxing), full moon, and last quarter (waning). What other kinds of rituals might you create to acknowledge the power of lunar rhythms for your own life? What does the moon have to say to your ongoing journey of discernment and deep listening to your heart's desires? What are you discovering about yourself as you immerse yourself in these sacred rhythms?

Phase

Ivory belly carved
to a sliver and then gone,
three days later, gleam of quartz
appears again among points
of silver fire, circling the sky
slowly like a white cow
in a summer meadow.

The moon is a poem
sometimes full in my mouth
summer's first strawberry
sometimes a communion
wafer dissolving on the tongue
sometimes she is gone
and I gulp at the air
thirsty for darkness.[2]

FIVE

Seasons of the Year

> The "velocity" involved in paying the bills is very different from the "velocity" of love-making, as most of us understand extremely well. The things we value most, we almost always try to do with some nimbus of timelessness around them: the opportunity to get lost and found again, to dissolve into what can feel like eternity.
>
> —Christian McEwen, *World Enough and Time*

We expand our focus from the lunar month to the seasons of the year. We shift our awareness from lunar cycles to solar ones. With this shift, you are encouraged in your daily life to be present to the changing of the seasons as doorways that are thresholds of invitation.

Spring is a dynamic time of blossoming, when the world begins to break open through the splendor of color. Summer is a season of fruitfulness and fullness, when the earth's bounty comes to her fullness and we are well nourished. Autumn enters into the great release of the earth, harvesting the gifts and releasing what is not necessary. Winter calls us into the grace of stillness and incubation, knowing the dark has her own wisdom that must be embraced before spring arrives again.

Each of us has a different relationship to the seasons shaped by memories and life experiences, which add other layers to the natural expressions I described. Our relation to seasons is also shaped by landscape and culture. In the Pacific Northwest, late winter is a time to see the gathering of thousands of geese and swans as part of their migration. In spring you can drive north to the Skagit Valley and see the Tulip Festival. In summer the days are especially long because of the high latitude and the tilting of the earth. Autumn is the time when the Native Americans celebrate the return of the great salmon to their birthplaces. Living in Ireland these last several years, I have become attuned to the rhythms of wild herbs growing: with snowdrops arriving as the very first sign of spring, hawthorn blossoms signaling the movement toward summer, the abundance of wildflowers growing in the Burren throughout summer, and then the blackberries, sloes (from the blackthorn), and haws (berries from the hawthorn) arriving with autumn. What are the signs of the seasons where you live?

Entering the Seasons

Spring

What are the words associated with springtime for you? Budding, blossoming, flowering, bursting, colorful, spectrum, pinks, reds, purples, oranges, that fresh green of new leaves?

Spend some time contemplating the meaning that spring has for you. Savor any memories evoked. Are there special events in spring, such as birthdays, anniversaries, or something new that arrives in the world around you? In Seattle, spring heralds the cherry blossoms, which was always a delight for me to witness—the arrival of the buds, the breaking forth of blossoms, and then the scattering of the petals like pink snow.

Make a list of words and associations you have for the season. Then give it your own name: *Spring is the season of . . .* (See if you can let this name emerge intuitively without thinking it through too much.)

Where in your life are you remaining tight in the bud? What is the risk of blossoming for you?

Summer

What are the words and images associated with summer for you? Bursting berries, lush roses, gleaming sunflowers, ice cream, heat rising, swimming, refreshment?

Spend some time contemplating the meaning that summer has for you. Savor any memories evoked. Are there special events in summer, such as birthdays, anniversaries, or something new that arrives in the world around you? Summer is often the season when a local farmers market returns. When we lived in Seattle, it ran through November, but that first weekend when the market returned and the community gathered to celebrate the joys of fresh, local, and sustainable food, my heart always felt joyful.

Make a list of words and associations you have for the season. Then give it your own name: *Summer is the season of . . .* (See if you can let this emerge intuitively without thinking it through too much.)

Where in your life is feeling most fruitful? What are you on fire for?

Autumn

What are the words and images associated with autumn for you? Leaves turning, release, surrender, fall, harvest, darkness growing, comfort food?

Spend some time contemplating the meaning that autumn has for you. Savor any memories evoked. Are there special events in autumn, such as birthdays, anniversaries, or something new that arrives in the world around you? In Seattle autumn is the season when the salmon return home to spawn. It is quite an amazing sight to see them swimming upstream by the hundreds to the exact place of their own birth. They die after giving birth, this last offering a sacrifice of their lives.

Make a list of words and associations you have for the season. Then give it your own name: *Autumn is the season of . . .* (See if you can let this emerge intuitively without thinking it through too much.)

Where are you longing to return to some essential self? What beautiful things would need to be flaked away and released to reveal it?

Winter

What are the words and images associated with winter for you? Frost, soup, snowy landscapes, hearth fires, long dark nights?

Spend some time contemplating the meaning that winter has for you. Savor any memories evoked. Are there special events in winter, such as birthdays, anniversaries, or something new that arrives in the world around you? Seattle and Galway winters are long and dark and wet. When we lived in California, the change in light was not as noticeable through the seasons as it is in other places, but the northern latitudes offer up many long hours to savor the gifts of darkness, often bringing lots of rain and reason to stay indoors and ponder.

Make a list of words and associations you have for the season. Then give it your own name: Winter is the season of . . . *(See if you can let this emerge intuitively without thinking it through too much.)*

We often think of winter as a season to get through as we wait for spring to arrive, eager for winter to be over. But what if we could honor it for its own integrity and depth? What if winter was simply a gift that we needed to unwrap slowly and with great care? What gift might that offer for your own journey of discernment?

Liturgical Rhythms

Sean O'Duinn, a Benedictine monk at Glenstal Abbey in Ireland, writes about the connections between the Celtic movement through the seasons and the Christian liturgical year in his book *Where Three Streams Meet*.[1] He describes the great Celtic wheel, which includes the four stations of the sun: the two solstices (summer and winter) and the two equinoxes (spring and autumn). At the solstices, the sun is farthest from the equator and seems to stand still (the word *solstice* comes from a Latin word meaning "to stand still"). At the equinoxes, the sun is over the equator, and day and night are equal.

This great wheel of the year is further divided by the cross-quarter days, which fall directly between the solstices and equinoxes and include Samhain (November 1), Imbolc (February 1), Beltane (May 1), and Lughnasa (August 1) in the northern hemisphere (in the southern hemisphere these are shifted by six months; for example, Samhain falls on May 1).

In his book, O'Duinn describes how the Christian feasts of our liturgical calendar became aligned with the great turning of the year: the winter solstice and the feast of Christ's birth, the summer solstice and the feast of St. John the Baptist's birth. The equinoxes align with the feasts of conception. The Annunciation, when Mary is called to say yes to bear the Christ child, is celebrated March 25 (nine months before Christmas and close to the vernal equinox), and similarly, the conception of John the Baptist, which is celebrated in the Byzantine Rite on September 24, is close to the autumnal equinox. The two great figures of the New Testament are intimately linked to the stations of the sun.

O'Duinn further goes on to explore the great Church feasts that coincide with the cross-quarter days. We celebrate All Saints and All Souls at Samhain, which recognizes the time when the veil is thin between heaven and earth and the dark half of the year begins. We honor the feast of St. Brigid and the Presentation of Christ in the Temple at Imbolc, the beginning of the earliest signs of spring and the agricultural year. The Easter season and Pentecost (which varies according to the lunar cycle) fall near Beltane, which also begins the bright half of the year. The feast of Christ's Transfiguration (August 6) falls near Lughnasa, which honors the firstfruits of the harvest.

Thresholds in Time

Each of these points on the wheel of the year offers us a threshold in time. A threshold space is a doorway into a new way of being, a new season of life, and a new invitation. If we are attentive to the turning of the seasons, we can discover their rhythms deep within our own hearts.

These moments call us to enter liminality, which means dwelling on the threshold in a state of unknowing, openness, ambiguity, and indeterminacy. Our identity and state of being is less defined. It is a time of transition where we let go of old understandings and welcome in new ones. Each season offers particular gifts, but we don't know exactly how they will unfold in our lives—that is, how the questions raised by the earth's turning will interact with our life story in this particular moment.

Imagine as you move through the year that with each moment of turning you are stepping across a new threshold, asking what this season reveals to you now. St. Teresa of Avila described the soul as an inner castle with concentric rooms. The spiritual journey consists in moving to new rooms of the soul. Each new season calls you deeper within.

The seasons help us into a different relationship to time. We begin to see—as we have with the rise and fall of the day, the preparation and rest of Sabbath, and the waxing and waning of the moon—that time has varying qualities. Each moment calls us to yield to its invitation, not striving or grasping at something other than what is being offered.

Consider creating ways to mark these eight turning points of the year honored in both earth-based and Christian traditions. You might simply take a day or afternoon of retreat to be out in creation and be present to the world's unfolding wisdom. Honor this crossing of a threshold in your life with poetry, art-making, or dance as ways of listening. Mark the dates of each new season on your calendar, and have a day or an afternoon of reflection to help you prepare to enter the new season and listen for the invitations being offered.

Scripture Reflection from John Valters Paintner

A Time for Everything
(Ecclesiastes 3:1-8)

> For everything there is a season, and a time for every
>   matter under heaven:
> a time to be born, and a time to die;
> a time to plant, and a time to pluck up what is planted;
> a time to kill, and a time to heal;
> a time to break down, and a time to build up;
> a time to weep, and a time to laugh;
> a time to mourn, and a time to dance;
> a time to throw away stones, and a time to gather stones
>   together;
> a time to embrace, and a time to refrain from embracing;
> a time to seek, and a time to lose;
> a time to keep, and a time to throw away;
> a time to tear, and a time to sew;
> a time to keep silence, and a time to speak;
> a time to love, and a time to hate;
> a time for war, and a time for peace.

–Ecclesiastes 3:1-8

Almost everyone has heard this particular passage from the Book of Ecclesiastes. It's easy to memorize and quote. It obviously relates to all sorts of situations. And then there's the song "Turn! Turn! Turn!" based on it, originally written by Pete Seeger in the fifties and made famous by The Byrds. With PR like that, how can it not be so widely known and loved?

But these verses are kind of a one-hit-wonder for a long and varied book of the Bible. Ecclesiastes is part of the Wisdom books and includes allegories, parables, proverbs, and narrative. And yet, despite all it has to offer, this book has a refrain that bookends the first and last chapters—"Vanity of vanities" (1:2 and 12:8).

It has been stated better by those smarter than myself that knowledge and wisdom begin with acknowledging what we don't know. And even when we think we have it all figured out, it changes. New information is presented and old assumptions must change. Life, like the seasons, can be quite fleeting. But therein lies its beauty.

As I mentioned in the last chapter, I didn't grow up knowing what proper seasons were. I thought I did. But the seasons of Sacramento Valley in California just went from nice weather to warmer nice weather and kind of stayed like that for most of the year. I didn't really have separate seasonal wardrobes or special winter coats. Some friends owned ski clothes, but with the ocean and mountains so close, one could go surfing in the morning and end one's day in the snow.

But speaking of coats, I was just as likely to carry a jacket with me in the summer as in the winter. You see, everyplace was air-conditioned—homes, businesses, cars. A lot of things can break or be run down on a car and it'd still work, but if the air-conditioning went out, no expense was spared to fix the sweatbox-on-wheels. Movie theaters were the worst. They'd always have the air-conditioning cranked up to meat-locker settings. You needed to bring some sort of coat or jacket or sweater so you could enjoy the film without shivering the entire time. And it just made going outside afterward unbearable. Stepping out into the blazing sun after a matinee was like getting slapped in the face with a wave of heat.

Ironically, where I live now in Ireland we have the opposite problem in winter. You need to bundle up in a couple of warm layers of clothes with a nice top coat to go out to meet your friends at the local pub for an evening out. But once you get there, you quickly realize that the heaters are on full-blast to fight the cold, the traditional turf fire is going to add a bit of ambience, and there are probably some people dancing to the music playing. In other words, you're in a small room with a lot of people, and you're all roasting with no place to put your coat.

In contrast to California and Ireland, Norway seems to have gotten it right. Christine and I visited a few winters ago to lead a retreat and discovered a beautifully gentle way of embracing the season at hand. Not only were most places not cranking the heat to maximum but also the lighting was muted. Most places we went had candles that were brighter than the outside, but in keeping with the softer mood that nature was creating, as it was near the winter solstice with only a few hours of the sun just poking above the horizon. It seemed to us they were trying not to fight the elements but to work in harmony with them. We could all learn a lesson from that.

This isn't to say that Ireland doesn't do the seasons justice, in general. I have certainly grown more aware of and appreciative of the different seasons as I have moved slowly northward in my life. Our move from California to Seattle, Washington, was a real eye-opener in regard to having actual seasons. The building we lived in was surrounded by cherry trees. I looked forward to them blooming every year, even if it was just for a week or two. I even loved the carpet of pink petals on the sidewalk that quickly turned to brown mush. The slow arrival of growing green leaves was a delight and welcome shade in the summer. Then came autumn, and as the days grew colder and the leaves began to fall and dance on the wind, the branches revealed their own beauty. Winter would sometimes bring snow that outlined the trees and invited us to rest, even if it was a forced pause because the roads were closed due to icy conditions. But once the snow melted, I knew that spring was on its way again and the cherry blossoms weren't far behind. The anticipation was half the fun.

If the trees had been pink all year, I doubt I would have appreciated it as much. That's what I've learned about life from the seasons: appreciate what is before me at the moment, for it will not last.

I know that may sound sad to some, as St. Benedict's instruction to "keep death before your eyes always"[2] may sound morbid. But it has cultivated a heart of gratitude in me that helps me appreciate the life I have now.

What is your favorite season, or seasonal transition, and what life lessons has it taught you? Or is there a season that you find particularly challenging? What lessons might you learn from it?

Practice: Slow Walking

One of my favorite spiritual practices is contemplative walking, which may be why it appears in most of my books. I believe, along with Wallace Stevens, that "perhaps / the truth depends on a walk around a lake."[3] Often when I feel stuck in a writing project or a poem, I need to step away and move my body to allow new insights to arise.

I love that my dog gets me out most days, even when the weather is less than ideal, which happens quite often in the west of Ireland. I have grown to love walking in the gentle rain when most others stay inside. There is a hush to the world.

One of my favorite parts of walking is paying attention to the signs of the season around me: the color of the leaves on the trees and the flowers in full bloom or withering late in the season. I have discovered tremendous grace from the simple act of paying attention through the year and slowly cultivating a deep trust in these fundamental rhythms of nature. Spring always follows winter, summer always comes around again, autumn reminds me of the beauty in dying and release, and winter always invites me into deep rest. The poet William Stafford described the world as offering us a perpetual "scripture of leaves."[4]

Slow walking has less to do with the pace at which you walk and more to do with the attention you bring to it. This isn't walking for fitness or to get somewhere. This is walking for pure presence and wonder at the world. If I am feeling sluggish or tired, a walk can help to awaken me and shift my energy so that I am attuned again to delight.

Try going for a slow walk where your sole purpose is to pay attention to the signs of the season around you. What do you notice and discover about the subtleties of the season? How does walking help you to discover new dimensions to the season you are in both internally and externally?

Meditation: Movement with the Seasons

The following is a modification of our meditation from chapter 1 on the four moments of the breath, but this time we will connect our movements to the seasons of the year. We will pause and listen to our bodies and our imaginations to see if we might bring an embodied response or symbolic gesture to symbolize the energy of each moment. The movement can be done while sitting in a chair or even lying down. Feel free to stand as well. You might want to play some music that encourages your body to begin to respond in movement as a way to enter into the meditation.

However you choose to have your body—sitting, standing, or lying down—allow a few moments to arrive to this posture and become aware of your breath. Sink into your body; feel the support of the floor beneath you. Notice if there are any places of tightness, and see if you can soften those with a gentle stretch or massage. Close your eyes and turn your gaze inward. This is a time for you to tune into your own inner movements. Trust whatever wants to emerge during this time of prayer, and allow it to flow through your body, simply making space for the full expression.

Now begin to slow your breath down and move into an awareness of the four parts of the breath—the moment of inhale, the pause between your inhale and exhale, the moment of exhale, and the pause between your exhale and inhale. Take a couple of breaths in which you are aware of all four moments in your breath, noticing the different quality each part has. Savor each moment slowly.

We're going to allow some time now to explore the felt quality of each of these four moments and connect them to the rhythms of the sun.

As you breathe, bring your focus to your inhalation and allow it to be slow and full. Imagine as you breathe in the blossoming forth of spring-time. As you repeat each breath cycle, hold that image in your heart on the inhale. Slowly begin to explore on the inhale any movement that reflects the quality of this flowering energy for you. You can use just your arms, or you can bring your torso or your whole body into the move-ment. As you play with this, begin to notice if there is a gesture prayer that is emerging for you to reflect the quality of inhalation and growth of springtime. Let yourself move through this a couple more times, and then come to rest in stillness again.

As you continue noticing your breath, shift your focus now to the moment between your inhalation and exhalation. Pause for just a moment between the inhale and exhale and notice how this moment of the breath feels in your body. Experience the fullness of life-giving oxygen in your lungs. As you repeat the breath cycle, begin to imagine the vibrant presence and fullness of summertime, and hold that image within you in this moment of physical expansion. Then slowly begin to explore in this experience of fullness; see if there is a movement that reflects the quality of summer's fruitfulness for you. Notice how your body wants to move, rather than thinking your way through this experi-ence. Just allow a posture or gesture to emerge, and give some space for exploring this. Then come to rest into stillness again.

Stay with the breath, but now bring your focus to your exhalation and allow it to be slow and full. As you breathe out, imagine the waning of autumn and release of leaves toward the quiet earth. As you repeat each breath cycle, hold this image on the exhale of waning. Then begin to notice if your body has a response that arises to the quality of this experience. Begin to play with the movement emerging, and see if there is a gesture to reflect this. Let yourself have this embodied experience, moving through it a couple of times and being present to what stirs in you in response. Then come to rest in stillness again.

Now we move to the final part of the breath. As you continue your breath cycles, bring your focus to the moment between exhalation and inhalation, and pause there with each breath. Experience the emptiness of breath as it leaves your body and you await that next inhale. As you allow yourself to rest for a moment in that place of discomfort and unknowing, imagine the dark nights of winter. Hold this image in your heart at the end of each cycle, and then begin to explore how your body wants to move in response to this experience. Open yourself to whatever gesture or posture might evoke for you an embodied expression of the energy of stillness and mystery. Take a few moments to explore this. Then come to rest in stillness again.

I invite you into one last movement through the four prayer stations of the breath. This time as you enter each one, bring the season to your imagination and offer the movement prayer that rose up in your initial exploration so that, as you move through the breath, you link these four gestures together in a kind of dance.

So as you breathe in, imagine the flowering forth of spring, and allow your body to embody a gesture to express this energy or quality. As you pause between inhale and exhale, imagine the fullness of summer's heat, and embody a gesture to reflect this energy or quality. As you exhale, imagine the yielding of autumn, and allow your body to express this in movement. And as you pause between exhale and inhale, imagine the stillness of winter, and notice how your body wants to move in response.

I invite you each night before bed to consider playing some contemplative instrumental music and enter into this breath and movement meditation. Let your gestures become an embodied prayer of gratitude for the wisdom of the seasons in your own life. Move through the cycles several times, and then rest at the end in stillness, noticing what you are experiencing in your body in response. Then open your heart to receive the gift of dreams.

Creative Exploration: Mandala of the Seasons

I invite you to create a mandala of the four seasons to explore in image, color, symbol, and shape the energies each of the seasons is calling you to consider now in your life.

Mandala is a Sanskrit word for "circle." It is a container for sacred awareness. Psychologist Carl Jung believed deeply in the need to create a holy and safe space to explore the center of our beings, and he saw the mandala as a symbol of this *temenos* (a sacred space that surrounds a temple or altar). He used the word *temenos* to describe the inner space deep within us where soul-making takes place. The sacred circle is the outer container for our inner exploration.

Set aside some sacred time and space to enter into this experience. I suggest two hours if possible. Begin by gathering the necessary supplies:

- Cardstock used to make a large circle or a cardboard cake round purchased from a baking supply store. You can make this any diameter you like, but I recommend a large-enough space to be able to work in four different quadrants of the circle. You might want to lightly draw the quadrants by using a pencil to create a cross across the center.

- Sources for your images. Use catalogs or magazines. If you don't have anything at home, consider purchasing a copy of *National Geographic* and just using one magazine as your source to limit your materials. You can also use colored paper such as construction paper or wrapping paper.

- Colored pencils or pens if you prefer to engage in this exploration through drawing in different colors rather than using collage materials

- Glue stick and scissors if you use collage materials

- Journal and pen

Create a sacred space for yourself by turning off the phone and computer, spreading out your supplies on a table or the floor, lighting a candle, putting on some meditative music, and allowing time to center yourself and breathe.

I invite you to enter into a time of art exploration of the seasons with this brief meditation to help you get centered in preparation.

Begin by connecting to your breath and becoming present to the four moments of your breath cycle. As you inhale, breathe in the flowering energy of spring, feel the new life being breathed into you. In the moment between inhale and exhale, feel the fullness of summer's fruitfulness in your body, alive with oxygen. As you exhale, breathe out the surrender of autumn and feel the release of old patterns and stories that no longer serve you. In the moment between exhale and inhale, feel the emptiness of winter and the call to stillness and rest. Move through several breath cycles, tending to this rhythm with an awareness of the seasons. Using your breath, draw your awareness down to your heart center, placing a hand on your heart to make a physical connection.

Once your body feels relaxed and open, begin to move toward the art supplies. Keep your awareness in your body, and allow your intuition to guide you. When you notice thoughts or judgments arising, return to your breath and let them go.

Allow the art process to be a journey of discovery. Release your desire or need to know how it will look. Even release your need to represent the seasons.

If you are making a collage, begin sorting through the images and create four piles, one for each of the seasons. You are not looking for images that directly depict each season, but images that evoke the quality of the season for you. As you find an image that stirs an emotional response in you, ask yourself which season it wants to be in, and place it in the pile without analysis or judgment. Simply trust the process.

Once you have several images in each pile, begin work on the mandala. I recommend working on each quadrant separately in their natural sequence. You can begin with any of the four seasons, but whichever one you are drawn to begin with, move through the other three in their natural order in a clockwise direction around the circle.

Paste the images for each season to their quadrant. If you are drawing instead of making a collage, begin to draw images that come to you to reflect each season.

As you begin each new quadrant, take a few moments to connect again to your breath, and pay special attention to the moment of breath that corresponds to the season. Imagine you are crossing a threshold as you enter into each new season's energy, inviting it to guide and shape your art exploration.

Allow about an hour for gathering your images into four piles reflective of the seasons and creating your mandala. Place the images in an intuitive way, noticing what feels satisfying.

Spend some time with your mandala just gazing upon it with soft and loving eyes. As with your discernment, this is not something for you to figure out but something to receive as gift. Be open as you let your eyes wander over the images, just noticing your inner experience.

After some time spent in this quiet receiving, take out your journal and begin by entering into an image on the mandala that is especially calling to you. Use your imagination to experience what it is like to be this image. Begin your writing with "I am ..." and then describe the feelings, textures, colors, shapes, and experiences of this image from inside of its voice.

Do this "I am ..." exercise for at least one image from each quadrant.

Then move into a time of dialogue between images. Select two images (one each from two different quadrants) and have them engage in conversation. What do they have to say to one another?

Spend some time reflecting on what each season is calling you to as reflected in the images that emerged in your collage.

Close your reflection with a time of honoring the gifts and insights you have received and offering gratitude for the wisdom of the seasons.

Mandala Movement Exploration

You can take this one step further and bring the seasons into your body. Prop up your mandala on a chair or somewhere you can stand in front of it and easily see it. Allow your gaze to fall on one of the images. Bring it into your body and notice how it feels. What shape or gesture feels like a physical reflection of the image? How would this image want to move if it were alive? Spend several minutes exploring the dance this image calls you to. Do this for one image in each seasonal quadrant.

Allow time at the end to move from one energy to another, experiencing a sequence and rhythm as you dance through the seasons.

Come to a resting place and put your hand on your heart. Bring your discernment to your awareness, and notice what wisdom your body offers.

Closing Blessing

What are you discovering about these larger solar cycles of the year? Which season do you find yourself in now? Which season do you resonate the most with, and which one do you resist? How might the seasons offer you wisdom for discernment in your life?

What are the memories you have of each season?

What are the cultural celebrations that offer another nuance to the seasons' gifts?

How are you being called to the flowering forth of spring?

Where in your life do you experience the fruitfulness of summer?

What do you need to release to make space for the rest and newness of autumn?

How are you being called into a time of deep listening and stillness of winter?

Seasons

Spring

Pink, white buds unfold
slowly on black branch tips
quivering at first
then thundering forth in a
riot of color, streamers.

Summer

Nectarine gladness
watermelon slab drips pink
purple peonies
generous summer banquet
how we long to linger here.

Autumn

Pears falling from sky
slush of red, green, and gold
blankets the ground
amber, ruby, citrine leaves
falling, even death is art.

Winter

You can rest now
says the earth, naked branches
tremor in winter's wind
fin and feather fly far off,
warm fur burrowed underground.[5]

SIX
Seasons of a Lifetime

> Slow down, our sages advise, slow all the way down to the
> pace of stone and shadow.
>
> —Diane Ackerman,
> *A Slender Thread: Rediscovering Hope at the Heart of Crisis*

We have spent the last five chapters paying attention to the rise and fall
of the world in its natural cycles, to its blossoming and releasing, to its
rhythms and how they might be gifts to us as we long to live a life in
alignment with our heart's deep desires. This chapter is about reflecting
on the rhythms of your life and looking at its wider arc as part of the
sacred rhythms of time.

Our life moves in seasons. In broad strokes, there are the seasons of
childhood, young adulthood, midlife, and elderhood, which correspond
to the natural seasons of spring, summer, autumn, and winter. However,
within each of these life phases or cycles, we may experience any of the
seasons depending on what is happening for us.

The Nature of Spiritual Tensions

As we have been exploring, all of creation follows certain rhythmic patterns. Just as the ocean tides ebb and flow, so does life. As the sun rises
and sets, as the moon waxes and wanes, life also comes and goes. The
reality of life's rhythms unfolds in the sacred process of our own jour-
neys. As we grow in our capacity to be present to the sacred in the rise
and fall of each moment, we discover that God's deepest quality is mystery, and the very nature of mystery fosters an experience of tension. Our
finite minds can only comprehend so much of spiritual reality, and so as
we mature spiritually, we are called upon to learn to live with a certain

measure of ambiguity and tension. Mystery is pregnant with hundreds of levels of unfolding, revealing, and concealing.

God is portrayed in scripture as transcendent and immanent, hidden and revealed, unknowable and knowable, unreachable and in our very midst. Our experience is likely that sometimes God seems very intimate and near, while at other times we feel estranged from the holy presence and God feels very far away.

When we encounter these tensions in our lives—perhaps the presence of joy and grief together or the tension between different desires in our discernment—we long for a sense of inner resolution, and yet the reality of our lives is that we will always live with some kind of tension. Sometimes the outer world is in the full blossom of spring while our inner life is still in the deepest dark of winter. Sometimes we feel the joy of spring and the grief of autumn at the same time, because life is offering to us both hope and loss, woven together.

Our call is to hold the full spectrum of our experience, honoring it all and allowing nature to be a wise guide in the process. The rhythms and cycles of the seasons help us to cultivate this capacity for full presence in the face of tension. We must resist the dualistic ways we have been trained to think in this culture and befriend the full range of what is happening in a given moment.

Transitions and Life Thresholds

All of the seasons of our lives are doorways across thresholds. Nature calls us to be fully present to the energy in transitional spaces and moments. I also learn to practice being present in these times through yoga. In my classes I am often reminded to be as mindful in the movement between poses as I am in the actual pose itself. The goal is not to get through a certain number of poses but rather to be as mindful as possible in the ones I do move through. So instead of rushing myself to the next thing, I become fully present to the moments between as well. This absolute attention to graceful transition, rather than a mindless and rushed movement, applies to the whole of my life. I bring this full attention not just to the activities of my day or the events of my life but also to those moments between them. Those places of transition are often especially filled with tension.

Twice now in my life I have sat vigil with a dying mother, with my own and with John's. During these threshold moments, time has an entirely different shape. It feels elastic, as if time were stretched out forever; and, at the same time, it dwells in the eternal now where nothing beyond us has any significance in that moment. These were truly the most graced experiences of my life. It is a profound gift to dwell at this threshold with another, journeying in community together to life's edges. Birth and death invite us into the most profound of these life thresholds.

In the last couple of years I have also been invited to hold the paradox of life's beginnings and endings together. As my father-in-law, John Paul, was dying, his grandson Hagen was being born. John Paul's funeral and Hagen's baptism were performed in the same service. It was a touching way to honor how life is always bringing us births and deaths at every moment. More recently I had two good friends experience the opposite thresholds of life: one was journeying with her husband through the final stages of Parkinson's and the other was getting ready to give birth to her first child.

I attended a Spiritual Directors International conference a few years ago, during which the conference spiritual director led the whole gathering in times of prayer. Several hundred bodies in a hotel ballroom does not lend itself easily to grace and stillness; however, when she asked us all to stand, she invited us to make that transition as absolutely slow and mindful as we could. I was struck in that moment by the way this simple movement from sitting to standing for prayer could itself be an act of intentionality, of moving through a threshold.

There are days when my schedule is full of appointments and meetings, and I rush from one thing to the next. These are the times when I am more likely to end up driving to save time rather than to walk or ride the bus. I am aware of how my sometimes rushed life leads me to make decisions that are harmful to the earth and to my own spirit. I usually try to keep a spaciousness to my day, but sometimes I try to fit in just one more thing, to squeeze more out of time than is warranted, and then my transitions become sloppier and mindless. I move to the next activity as a goal rather than tending the whole process. And usually this leads to feeling disconnected from myself and my deeper desires.

This is how important our relationship to time can be. We are called to cultivate patterns and ways of being that nourish a slow soulfulness and mindful attention to all that is unfolding.

I bring these questions to the seasons of my life: Are there places where I move mindlessly on from one life stage to another? From one season to another in my rush to get to the next thing or project? Or can I be absolutely present to the movement between things and discover there a grace and wonder that was previously hidden?

In considering my intention, specifically when practicing yoga, I ask myself: What do I want my practice to embody today? How do I want to be in the world? How does my true self move through each moment?

Each breath, each transition, each pose, and each rest becomes an invitation into awareness and wholeness.

What Is It the Season For?

Years ago when I lived in Berkeley, California, I had a wonderful spiritual director who would often ask me this simple question when I was in the midst of discernment: "What is it the season for?" It was a profoundly freeing question because it honored the fact that my life had varying seasons, times when certain things were called for and other things needed to be released. At the time I was in graduate school finishing my PhD studies, and I often had to remind myself that I needed to direct the majority of my attention and time to them if I was ever going to finish.

After my mother died, I entered into a deep period of grief, and one of the things I found great comfort in was something a dear friend who was also a rabbi told me. She said that in Jewish tradition, in that first year after a significant loss, nothing extra is expected of the person. What a beautiful gift she offered to me by reminding me that this was a season of grief, and taking on new projects would not be honoring where I was. Similarly, in periods of my life when I have experienced a flare of my autoimmune illness, I have to ask whether the tasks I want to take on would be honoring my illness, in order to remind myself of a call to focus on healing.

As someone who often feels inspired by many possible projects, I return to this question again and again of whether the project honors what I am currently capable of even in times of wellness and joy. Perhaps especially as I reach midlife and my awareness of the limitations of my time left start to feel even more acute, this question invites me to remember what is most valuable in this moment right now. Another season might call for something else, but I am invited to turn to what wants to come to ripeness right now.

Scripture Reflection from John Valters Paintner

Seasons of Jesus' Lifetime

The Birth of Jesus (Luke 2:1-7)
The Boy Jesus in the Temple (Luke 2:41-52)
The Baptism of Jesus (Matthew 3:13-17)
The Temptation of Jesus (Matthew 4:1-11)
The Wedding at Cana (John 2:1-12)
Jesus Washes the Disciples' Feet, and the New
    Commandment (John 13:1-20; 31-35)
The Death of Jesus (Mark 15:33-41)

Since no one point in time can encapsulate anyone's lifetime, let alone that of Jesus, for this reflection we will be looking at several key stories throughout his life.

There are two rather different infancy narratives, but I chose the story of Jesus' birth from the Gospel of Luke because it is perhaps more relatable to most people than Matthew's narrative. There's no courtly intrigue between government officials and foreign dignitaries. What we have is a simple family dealing with a bureaucratic obligation at an already stressful time. But as parents have always done, they dealt with the hand they were given and did the best they could.

Even the facts that they were surprised to find out they were expecting and that they had visitors after the birth are unremarkable.

We don't learn much of anything about Jesus' childhood. It's not until his early adolescence, a year before he would have had his bar mitzvah at thirteen, that anything truly remarkable happens: Jesus rebels, sort of. After the family's yearly pilgrimage to the Holy City, the boy stays behind. It takes his parents, who were traveling separately because of cultural norms at the time, a day to realize he was even missing. Mary probably assumed that Jesus decided to travel with Joseph and the other men for the first time, and Joseph probably assumed Jesus was still traveling with his mother. It takes them three days to find young Jesus, alive and well, just hanging out in the Temple, teaching the elders. It wasn't so much teenage rebellion as his first step in self-actualization, even if he was doing his Father's work. But he was doing it because he wanted to. The story ends by stating that after this Jesus just grew in maturity and wisdom, nothing remarkable. But much was going on.

There are many theories about the missing eighteen years of Jesus' life between this incident at the Temple and the beginning of his public ministry. Suffice it to say that Jesus doesn't go out on his own for many years, and there are two significant stories that mark his transition into independence.

The first is Jesus' baptism by his cousin John at the Jordan River. John initially refused to baptize Jesus, stating that their roles should be reversed for the ritual. But Jesus insisted, saying that the ritual was important—someone else had to perform the rite and it had to be publicly witnessed. Only once this is done is Jesus blessed by the Holy Spirit.

In the next chapter of Matthew's gospel, Jesus goes alone into the desert for private reflection and preparation. It is here that Jesus is tempted, first to abuse his power to feed himself, then to test God's protection of him, and finally to rule over all the world. Even though these temptations come from an outside source, they all appeal to Jesus' inner struggle. In testing his own strength and refusing to give in, Jesus is finally ready to begin his public ministry.

Jesus' first public miracle is at a private wedding in Cana and at the behest of his mother. Shortly after recruiting his twelve disciples, mainly hardy fishermen and laborers, Jesus brings them to a wedding where the bride and groom run out of wine (perhaps because Jesus arrives with twelve extra guests). Then what follows is something that I believe to be one of the best examples of prayer in the Bible. Mary turns to Jesus and points out the dilemma to her son. She does not tell him what to do. She doesn't even ask him to do anything. Mary simply points out the problem and, in her last recorded words in the gospels, tells the servants, and all of us who will later read her powerful words of faith in Jesus: "Do whatever he tells you." It isn't Jesus' flashiest miracle or his largest crowd, but his disciples come to believe in him and word quickly spreads.

There is much that happens to Jesus along the way from his first miracle to his death in Jerusalem, but we will skip all that to focus on the end of his journey. His final days include another dinner party (something he partook in often throughout his ministry). But this last supper of Jesus is a bit more intimate, with just his closest disciples, many of whom were with him at the wedding in Cana. In John's gospel, we have the beautiful and moving story of Jesus getting on his hands and knees to wash the feet of his dearest friends. Of course, Peter resists at first, only to then request to have the rest of him washed. What I love best about this story is that after Jesus is done, he turns to them and says, "I give you a new commandment, that you love one another. Just as I have loved you, you also should love one another" (Jn 13:34). Unlike the other gospels where Jesus commands us to love others as we love ourselves (a subjective measure that many struggle with), here Jesus gives the example of humility and service. He shows them, and us, how to love and tells them to do the same for others. It is an important final stage in Jesus' life and ministry as he passes the torch to the apostles to follow in his way.

I certainly won't be comparing my life with that of Jesus. But we all have highlights, milestones along our journey, and these are mine.

My parents were excited, anxious even, that I was born on the Feast of John the Baptist. After two much-loved daughters, they were hoping for a boy to name after my father, John Paul, so they were delighted that I was born with a little over an hour to spare on June 24. They told me many times how the doctor barely had time to scrub up and rush into the delivery room, his surgical gown still untied in the back. (I'm sure the nurses could've handled the delivery just fine without him, but it makes for a dramatic ending to several false starts over the previous week.) The emphasis on the feast day and sharing my father's name became central to my personal identity and connection to the church.

There were plenty of important moments in my first two decades, but my first real step toward personal autonomy came at the World Youth Day in Poland in 1991. I was going to college and working part-time, but I wasn't much changed from my teenage self. When the opportunity came to attend a gathering of Catholic young people from across the globe, I jumped at the chance. I admit my first motivation was to spend two weeks in Europe with my friends, but when I heard Pope John Paul II challenge us not to be afraid to be holy, something changed for me. Nothing outwardly changed in regard to my religion or school or work, but I had a newfound ownership of my faith that informed and inspired me (even if I'm still learning what it means to "be holy").

That moment of going from passive religiosity to active faith led me to my involvement with the Newman Center where I met Christine. Over the course of several months and a few retreats together we became friends. Then one night while discussing the trials and tribulations of dating other people, we realized we should date each other. To say it was one of the most significant realizations and changes to my life would be an understatement of biblical proportions.

Marrying Christine was the best decision I've ever made. And while life has been very good for us, over our twenty-five years of marriage we've faced the illness and death of all four of our parents. Not too long after our wedding, Christine's father was the first to die suddenly. And while that was a shock, the death of Christine's mother a few years later was a much deeper blow. My parents, particularly my mother, were a comfort during these times of loss. But when she was diagnosed with Alzheimer's and my father with Parkinson's, life changed again. We were living a couple of states away from my folks at the time, with my sister as their primary caregiver, but their declining health became a major factor in many life decisions. And even though I had far more warning than Christine did that my parents were going to die, the grief when they passed was still very real. We suddenly felt alone in the world with only each other for support. Sure, we had other family and friends, but there's something about finding oneself an orphan (even as an adult) that puts life in perspective.

The death of my mother was a contributing factor to my decision to move to Europe. My father was still alive, but we had never been so close that a move out of the country would have changed our relationship any more than my move out of state had done. Not only did we have his blessing to go but also we inspired him to move closer to the sea. But the move to Europe was huge. We sold our home and most of our possessions and, while we had the option of returning to the States, we had no plans to do so. We didn't even have much of a plan of what we'd do once we arrived. The fact that I couldn't establish residency in Austria and so had to move to Ireland is an indication that we didn't have everything figured out before we left. And while we are far more established now, owning our home and with me applying for Irish citizenship, we still don't know what life holds for us in the future.

What are three or four key points in your lifetime? How have you approached these times of change?

Practice: Slow Discernment

Often when we are in a period of not knowing what next steps to take in our lives we feel impatient. We want to rush to the answer, to have clarity and a sense of revelation.

For our fiftieth year of life, John and I were able to take a year of sabbatical. It took a lot of planning as we don't have institutional support and are responsible for raising all of our own funding. But the promise of a Jubilee felt really important, especially as I was feeling in need of some time for discernment, to listen to the life patterns that would nourish and support me best going forward.

It was such an act of trust to step into our Jubilee year and allow myself to have periods of time where I wasn't doing anything: wasn't working toward deadlines, wasn't trying to produce anything. I wanted the clarity and answers that I was searching for to come quickly in this year so I could set to work during the rest of the sabbatical implementing my new awareness. But much like the slow unfolding of Earth's seasons, our life seasons take their own time as well. Trying to rush ourselves to some premature awareness or insight does nothing to honor the needs of the soul for space and time to incubate.

If you are in the midst of a time of discernment and wondering what is next in your life, see if you might begin with letting go. Let go of your need to figure things out. Let go of a particular timetable (even if there are external time pressures). Let go of your own need to keep busy to move things along.

One of the best things I did for myself during our Jubilee year was to intentionally give myself time to not do anything at all. It felt very uncomfortable at times to have this extended period of not working toward anything, but I was able to lean into a deep trust that things were still at work within me. The book I wrote on Celtic spiritual practices is titled *The Soul's Slow Ripening* because my experience is that all the most fruitful life thresholds and transitions come about when we honor the soul's need for as much time as it takes to come to insight. There is no rushing the process forward. Learning to be in the discomfort of not knowing is a great gift. We cultivate humility when we acknowledge that some things are bigger than we are.

Meditation: Reflecting on the Seasons of Your Lifetime

Our souls have their own rhythm and pattern. Tending to the cycles of creation can offer us tremendous wisdom, but examining the seasons of our own souls can be equally fruitful.

Take some time with your journal and draw a timeline of your life. This could be in a literal "line," or perhaps you might represent your life in a spiral or other shape that resonates. Move into a contemplative and reflective space and, beginning with your earliest memories until the present day, move through your life experience in your imagination. As your life unfolds before you, make note about which season you were in during a given period of your life and when the transition came that thrust you into a new season. This is a way of giving honor to the seasons as they have actually unfolded in your life and the transitions that have ushered in a new experience or awareness. Notice if there are any patterns to the way the seasons have unfolded for you or any new awareness that comes from looking at your life in this way.

What were the moments of transition and letting go? When were the great celebrations? When did you hold vigil? When did you touch eternity? When did you say yes to life's call to risk and adventure? When did you hold back? When have been the seasons of activity and achievement, and when have been the seasons of letting go and releasing?

You might deepen into this experience by moving into a *lectio divina* practice with your life experiences. Ultimately the practice of *lectio divina* invites us to consider how we might read each moment as shimmering with sacred presence. As you create your timeline, consider practicing *lectio* with each significant event and allowing this process to take several days.

Lectio with Life Experience

Settling and Shimmering

Begin your time of prayer by deciding which life experience you want to focus on. Having created a timeline of your life, choose one of the threshold times to focus on in this prayer experience.

Allow some time for you to settle in to your chair and sink into your body. Become aware of your breathing, gently deepening it. As you inhale, imagine the breath of God filling not just your body but also the whole of your life with enlivening energy. As you exhale, imagine letting go of whatever keeps you from being fully present to life.

Allow your breath to carry your awareness down to your heart center. Rest in this space for a few moments, perhaps resting your hand on your heart and relishing the rhythm of your heartbeat, which sustains your life.

Savoring and Stirring

Begin to "read" your experience. In your imagination, walk through this experience, noticing where your attention is being drawn and welcoming in whatever memories or feelings arise. Move through the time of your life in an open-hearted and spacious way, and notice if there is a particular moment that wants some more attention. Listen for how your heart is being led. Make room within you to allow this moment to unfold in your imagination. Savor the sense experience of it. What do you remember of sight, smell, taste, touch, and sound? Are there images, colors, or symbols rising up into your awareness? Be present to the feelings that are being stirred, and welcome them in.

Summoning and Serving

Begin to shift your awareness and open yourself to the ways God was present to you in this experience. Is there a sense of how you are being called in your life to respond to this moment? What action or awareness is emerging from your reflection on this time?

Slowing and Stilling

Gently release everything that has been stirring in you. Connect to your breath again and allow the rhythm of your breath to fill you with peace. Let go of words and images so you can rest fully into a few moments of contemplative presence. Give yourself some time simply to be, remembering that your life is about more than the sum of your experiences and what you do in the world. Then release even this awareness and come to a place of deep stillness.

When you are ready to complete this time of prayer, allow your breath to gently bring your awareness back to the outer space of your room. Take some time to journal about what emerged in your prayer experience, writing about the moment that called for more attention.

Creative Exploration: Keep an Almanac of Your Life

The *Farmers' Almanac* tracks weather, astronomical observations, and other data so people know the best times to plant. In a similar way, begin to collect information about each week, month, and season in your own life as you move through them, noticing when your peak times of energy are and when you need more time for solitude and reflection.

Here are some things you might want to take note of:

- Special dates such as birthdays and anniversaries of marriages, deaths, other significant events
- Holidays and holy days that are significant for you
- What is happening in nature
- Sabbath days, moon cycles, and thresholds into seasons as possible days of retreat

This is not an activity you will necessarily complete in one sitting; however, you can begin by making some reflective time to listen for what rhythms you most want to cultivate in your life. How might your relationship to time shift through your growing awareness? Create short rituals to honor each of these events.

What happens when you let your life be shaped by its own organic rhythm?

Closing Blessing

Allow time to imagine the expansiveness of your heart and how it can hold both fullness and emptiness, the rise and fall of everything. Make space within to be present to life's tensions and paradoxes, and imagine the seasons as a wisdom text about how to live with grace in their presence.

Do you feel yourself ripening? Do you feel the sacred presence reaching out to you through the cycles of the world?

What are you discovering?

Life Cycles

Right now somewhere
someone is being born
skin tender and wet
lung bellows tested
hungry mouth reaches
while choirs of gorse
on the hillside sing.

Someone somewhere right
now is dying, skin slack,
bones press forward,
sister and son bedside
weeping for brevity,
council of trees creak
like an old door closing.

Sometimes the journey between
birth and death is a flash,
mouse fleeting across
the cold floor, cat's hot breath.

Sometimes life is long
a barrel of wine
in the cool cellar
for many summers
until one day
glasses are lifted
and clink,
warmth spreads

through the body slowly
like the lavender dawn.

When I was a child I filled
my pockets with springtime,
daffodils, bits of nest, a robin's egg.

Now I gather my treasures
like dandelion seeds
into my open hands,
close my eyes and blow.[1]

SEVEN

Ancestral Time

Now the dead move through all of us still glowing. . . .
What has been plaited cannot be unplaited.

—May Sarton, "All Souls"

Our Western culture doesn't make much room for the honoring of ancestors or valuing what a connection to the stories of our past might bring
to us. When we uncover the stories of those who have lived before us
for generations, though, we begin to understand ourselves better. Some
of these stories we may know the details of, and some we may have to
access and experience in an intuitive way. These memories live inside of
us, waiting for us to give them room in our lives. Making space in our
lives to learn our family history, to know some of the struggles and joys
of our ancestors, and to experience the land they walked on all gives us
a sense of time as generational and how things in our lives both were
planted by past generations and are planted for the generations to come.

We have scientific evidence through the work of epigenetics that
family wounds are carried unconsciously from generation to generation. The stories and traumas of our grandmothers and grandfathers are
our stories. We can help to heal the wounds of the past, and in the process heal ourselves, by telling those stories again—giving voice to the
voiceless, unnamed secrets and to the celebrations, insights, and wisdom
gathered over time.

Landscape, language, and culture have all shaped the stories we've
told, the words used to express the most aching sorrow and the most
profound joy. Ancestral lands with their trees, rivers, oceans, and undu-
lations have been imprinted on our psychic lives and our souls. Learning

some of the language our ancestors spoke or walking in the landscape that shaped them can bring us home to ourselves again.

Carl Jung and the Ancestors

Psychologist Carl Jung wrote extensively about the collective unconscious, which is this vast pool of ancestral memory within each of us; it is a kind of deposit of ancestral experience lived out over time. He believed it comprises the psychic life of our ancestors right back to the earliest beginnings. This means that nothing is lost; all of our ancestors' stories, struggles, and wisdom are available to us. Each of us is an unconscious carrier of this ancestral experience, and part of our journey is to bring this to consciousness in our lives.

He even believed the collective unconscious comprises our animal ancestry, the creatures we evolved from, which have existed longer than humans. The collective unconscious is the place where archetypes emerge—those symbols and experiences that appear across time and cultures. The stories of our ancestors are woven into the fabric of our very being.

In his book *Memories, Dreams, Reflections,* Jung wrote:

> I became aware of the fateful links between me and my ancestors. I feel very strongly that I am under the influence of things or questions which were left incomplete or unanswered by my parents and grandparents and more distant ancestors. It often seems as if there were an impersonal karma within a family, which is passed on from parents to children. It has always seemed to me that I had to answer questions which fate had posed to my forefathers, and which had not yet been answered, or as if I had to complete, or perhaps continue, things which previous ages had left unfinished.[1]

When we let these lost voices speak through our own lives, perhaps we will discover that our own deepest longings are woven together with theirs. Consider spending some time in your journal holding this image of offering space for the voices of your ancestors to speak. What stories might they tell? What wisdom might they offer?

Fate and Destiny

Michael Meade is a storyteller and mythologist who writes about the concepts of fate and destiny in ways that make a lot of sense to me. Rather than imagining these as fixed, predetermined realities, he explains fate as the set of agreements your soul makes before you enter the world to live within a certain family system and a particular time and culture.[2] All of us have to work with the wounds handed on to us, but in his view, our destiny—that which is our soul's deepest calling—actually emerges from the fate we live with in terms of family life. The particular kind of woundedness we must navigate actually has what we need to break open the treasure within us. He says that we may spend our lives running from our "issues" rather than listening to them as exactly the place where we may learn what we need to respond in fullness to the world. Whether or not the idea of "fate and destiny" resonates with you, I find it compelling to imagine that what I have had to deal with in my own brand of family wounding and angst is exactly what will break open my greatest gifts.

Murray Bowen was a psychiatrist in the twentieth century who developed eight concepts about how anxiety is dealt with in relationship systems.[3] For our purposes here, the most important of these concepts is the Multigenerational Transmission Process.

Bowen's central idea is that patterns of relationship are transmitted from generation to generation, and once you become aware of the ways your family system has operated, you can change the system by not participating in the established responses to anxiety. This work has applications to larger systems of relationships as well and has been used in congregations and to help pastors deal in healthy ways with community members rather than falling into their own established relationship patterns.

Through the concept of Multigenerational Transmission Process, Bowen believed that relationship patterns and anxiety are passed down genetically and that an essential part of the work of developing healthier relationships is to establish relationships with as many living family members as possible to hear their stories. One level of this work that has captivated me the most is the idea of our sacred stories being woven into a much larger tapestry of the generations that came before. We live in a very individualistic culture where not much honor is given to our ancestors and very little attention is paid to the stories that ripple through our very genetic code from generations that have gone before. Like Bowen, I recognize that our stories are embedded within the multiple layers of ancestral stories, the larger cultural stories of which they are a part, and then even more broadly, the sacred story of the earth and the cosmos.

I am affected in a profound way by the strands of these stories—my ancestry can be traced back through four main lines: Austria and Latvia on my father's side and Puritan New England (the 1600s) and England (before the 1600s) on my mother's side. Through this work, I can see how the trauma of war ripples through time, especially World War II for my father and World War I and the Civil War on my mother's side, because family members were killed in both.

One reflection on the influence of ancestral stories on a person' life is depicted in the film *Into the Wild*. It tells the true story of Christopher McCandless's journey away from the dysfunction of his parents toward the solitary promise of Alaska. It is an alluring theme; who of us has not experienced the pain that our families can wreak upon us and not flirted with the idea of running far, far away? In Bowen Theory, this is called "emotional cut-off," and this is a dominant cultural phenomenon. With greater possibilities for mobility than ever before, we can run farther and farther away from the things that scare us or have hurt us. We cut ourselves off emotionally or geographically or both.

I appreciated this film because it dealt with this impulse very honestly. A young man sets off to escape from the trauma of a difficult family after satisfying their hopes that he would graduate from college. His father is played beautifully by William Hurt, a man filled with rage and pain doled out onto those he loves.

I could identify with Christopher's longing to leave that pain behind, to go in search of a place where he did not have to deal with the messiness of human relationships. In fact, several months before my father died, I cut off all communication with him because of his emotional abuse. I would not stand for it any longer, and I still do not regret the choice I made for self-protection. It was important for me to be finally able to say that I demand to be treated with respect and care. In the wake of my father's death all those years ago, I felt relief and freedom; I felt like I could keep running in the other direction as far away from his compulsions as I could.

Then when I discovered the work of family systems theory, I became entranced by its power. It tells us not to run in the other direction but to run right back into the family system to understand it better. However, it also says to do so from a place of calm observance. Understand the anxiety patterns that have developed over generations so you don't have to engage them anymore. You no longer need to react from old wounds. This work of returning to the family system demands courage to face the full legacy of our family stories, with all of their joy and sorrow. And when you reenter the system from this perspective, the system itself begins to change.

I began to see my own ancestral history as a river of time flowing toward me. Seven generations back is not so very long ago. Thinking about the joys and traumas of my ancestors helped me to feel connected to the time of history and events I can only read about in books.

I am not like my father in so many ways, but his story is woven into my own. And of course, he left me with many gifts as well. I carry the grief and pain of his having to flee the country of his upbringing for another land at a formative age during World War II, a story he would never utter. Knit into my being are the unfulfilled longings that propelled him forward and the wounds that haunted him. It is my responsibility to begin narrating these sacred ancestral stories with a tenderness and care for the traumas they hold. In telling them again, I am weaving a thread through time.

At the end of the film, the protagonist is dying out in the Alaskan wilderness. In his journal he scrawls the words "happiness never shared is not real," and as he releases his hold on life, there is an image of him running toward his parents in the brilliant sunlight. In his imagination, he runs right into their arms and receives their embrace.

For some viewers, this might seem like a romanticized notion of reconnecting with family influenced by hallucination and starvation, especially in light of his father's abuse. However, for me it was a perfect moment, in a way film can express, that claims this truth I have come to understand: We simply can't run away from the pain of our families.

We can't escape the drama and dysfunction of human relationships. We carry an ancestral narrative in our bones and sinews, which are studded with these tales. Our task is *not* to forgive and forget, nor to act as though the abuse perpetrated is not important. Our task *is* to walk calmly and courageously back into that system.

Both of my parents have died and I have no siblings, so for me, I reach out to other family members, I walk again in formative landscapes and look with new eyes, and I enter back into my imagination and listen with new ears for what is happening. I gaze at photos of family members, looking for clues about their stories. I read books about the cultural stories that have shaped my ancestors. I honor this web that I am woven into and the way time connected me back through generations.

The call of this work is to walk back into the family system and embrace the reality of what *is*, asking why, and looking on it as an essential part of yourself: What of this ancestral narrative have I disowned that calls to me to be reclaimed?

Scripture Reflection from John Valters Paintner

The Genealogy
of Jesus the Messiah

(Matthew 1:1-17)

An account of the genealogy of Jesus the Messiah, the son of David, the son of Abraham.

Abraham was the father of Isaac, and Isaac the father of Jacob, and Jacob the father of Judah and his brothers, and Judah the father of Perez and Zerah by Tamar, and Perez the father of Hezron, and Hezron the father of Aram, and Aram the father of Aminadab, and Aminadab the father of Nahshon, and Nahshon the father of Salmon, and Salmon the father of Boaz by Rahab, and Boaz the father of Obed by Ruth, and Obed the father of Jesse, and Jesse the father of King David.

So all the generations from Abraham to David are fourteen generations; and from David to the deportation to Babylon, fourteen generations; and from the deportation to Babylon to the Messiah, fourteen generations.

—Matthew 1:1–6a, 17

This genealogy is often skipped over by most modern readers. It's not very exciting. Most of the people mentioned aren't even well-known biblical figures. And even I just left out ten and a half verses of the genealogy to conserve space and get on with my reflection. But at the time of its writing, all these verses were very important to set up what was about to be revealed.

The primary audience for the Gospel of Matthew was Jews. Not that Gentiles were excluded from the Good News of the Messiah, but this particular gospel account makes the case that Jesus of Nazareth is the long-awaited Messiah foretold in the Hebrew Scriptures. Who Jesus is in the Gospel of Matthew depends heavily on who his people are—that is, on his family lineage.

To that end, Matthew's first chapter is dedicated to genealogically linking Jesus to King David. It's interesting to note that the first verse mentions Abraham (the first person, along with his wife, Sarah, to make a covenant with Yahweh) and David, but King David gets mentioned first. The reversal of chronological order is not accidental. David is the key of this genealogy because it is from his house that the prophets say the Messiah will come. And so it is very important to make each link in the chain from Abraham to David to Jesus to prove that Jesus is the Messiah.

Tracing one's family tree has become quite popular lately. There are even television shows dedicated to this topic, usually celebrities getting professional help to discover their ancestors. Christine has done quite a lot of work on her own family tree, and I've looked into mine. I've traced my father's line back to the village in Germany from which they emigrated in the 1880s. Unfortunately, my mother's line dead-ends in Ireland because of poor record-keeping at the time and because of an ancestor who lied about his age (assuming he knew for sure) in order to book passage to America or to get a job once he arrived.

That's not to say I don't know anything about my family. There are stories that have been passed down through the generations, such as how my Bavarian ancestors decided to immigrate to America after they served in the German military and were harshly treated by the Prussian officers. My father once told me that his great-grandfather and his platoon were ordered to stand on a bridge by an officer who threw their pay into the river below and then ordered them to jump into the icy water to retrieve it. On my largely Irish mother's side of the family, one of my great-great-great-great-grandmothers was a Mohawk Native American, and she was given the name Mary while in the Catholic orphanage. (I don't know why she was there, but I am sure something very tragic happened to her family or tribe and that it probably wasn't accidental.)

And while I can point out that both sides of my family came from Europe after slavery was abolished in America, I can hardly say my family's hands are clean of the national crime of racism. Both families first settled in lands that would have originally been occupied by indigenous people. More recently, Christine and I own our home through the help of our families, who benefited from what we now know were racist practices in the real-estate industry. We started halfway up the property ladder to which others were denied access. None of us are only victims or oppressors. But if we don't acknowledge the sins of the past as much as we celebrate the accomplishments of our ancestors, then we can never break free of that cycle. We don't necessarily need to know all the details of the past to understand it and to learn from it.

Knowing all the individuals in one's family tree isn't necessary to feel a connection to the past. Whether or not we know how we are connected, we are still connected. Whether you can trace your family tree back dozens of generations or you're an orphan who doesn't even know your birth parents, we're all part of the same human family. We're all here now because of those who have come before us.

Actually being related to people doesn't even necessarily make one a family. Families sometimes, unfortunately, break apart. And there are many forms of nontraditional families. One of the early decisions of the Church was to welcome and incorporate Gentiles into becoming followers of the Jewish Messiah. Churches today certainly have a mandate to continue this tradition of radical hospitality. Faith is universal and not limited by bloodlines.

Family is also not limited by geography. It seems my sisters and I live farther and farther apart the older we get. Ironically, we're closer now despite our physical distance than when we lived together as children and fought all the time. Again, this plays out in the catholic (small C) church. We are universal, as God is omnipresent.

But God is not only everywhere; God is every-when. If we are united through faith to people on the other side of the globe, surely we are united through faith to people across time. This is the great "cloud of witnesses" (Heb 12:1), as near to us today as our relatives who are just a Skype call away.

What are some links (tangible or intangible) that you have to your ancestors?

Practice: Slow Travel and Ancestral Pilgrimage

One of my primary spiritual practices these last few years has been making ancestral pilgrimages. A pilgrimage is a journey of meaning to a sacred site—in this case, a place that was significant for my ancestors. I have traveled to my ancestral places of New England, England, Austria, and Latvia, some multiple times, as a part of my personal journey. These trips are a chance to experience slow travel, which means we are not tourists who want everything to happen according to a schedule. Instead, we are pilgrims who allow things to unfold according to their own timing.

A pilgrimage is a special kind of journey, one taken to a holy place with the hope for an encounter with the sacred and the intention of being changed by what happens both there and along the way. We don't go on pilgrimages to return the same person. This is especially true for an ancestral pilgrimage. I believe we are profoundly connected to the land and culture and stories of our ancestors in ways we often don't fully realize. Their experiences, sorrows, and joys are knit into our bones, woven into the fabric of our very bodies. The impulse to discover one's story often leads us to reach far back into history. We can't fully understand the impact of these connections until we stand on the land and speak the language of those who came before us and gave us the gift of life.

Pilgrimages take preparation. There are, of course, the practical details of planning a trip, which include buying maps and guidebooks and making an itinerary and reservations. But there is another whole level of preparation that also needs to take place, which includes reading the history of a place, learning some of the language, and preparing our hearts for an encounter with new stories. We are transformed both in the preparation process and on the journey itself.

I love the image and metaphor of pilgrimage. We often talk about our "life journey" because it conveys so well the process of our spiritual unfolding. There is a sense of movement to this image that honors the dynamism of God, a sense of movement that we experience in a pilgrimage. Pilgrimages also honor the power of physical places to change us and are thus deeply incarnational practices.

When I stood on the shores of the Baltic Sea in Latvia and imagined my father playing as a child in the sand and the waves, I connected to him as the boy he once was, loving the sea. I understood him in new ways. I saw the innocence of a young boy before the war came and shattered everything he knew.

In Phil Cousineau's *The Art of Pilgrimage*, he writes, "If your journey is indeed a pilgrimage, a soulful journey, it will be rigorous. Ancient wisdom suggests if you aren't trembling as you approach the sacred, it isn't the real thing. The sacred, in its various guises as holy ground, art, or knowledge, evokes emotion *and* commotion."[4] Cousineau looks at the mythical and symbolic qualities of pilgrimage and then invites the reader to consider ways to prepare for this journey through ritual and imagination as well as ways to engage in the journey itself, not as a consumer of experience, but as a seeker of the sacred. He also points to the pilgrimage as a microcosm of life—walking our path with reverence and expectation of holy encounter. Each time I prepare for the journey with excitement and anticipation, I also experience fear and trembling, knowing I will have to confront some shadow sides of my family system and myself. But it is in facing the dark depths that I no longer have to live in fear of them.

A pilgrimage doesn't have to be a long journey overseas. It might be to a nearby cemetery or a phone call with a living relative to ask about stories you have never heard before. But it begins with a dream and a longing; then the vision for how it will come to be unfolds slowly over time. Pilgrimage gives us a sense of the vastness of our ancestors spreading back both through time and across the land.

Meditation: Calling on the Ancestors

In this meditation experience I invite you into prayerful awareness and intention. You will want to have one or more unlit candles and a lighter available as part of the experience, perhaps on a home altar.

Begin by finding a quiet and comfortable space, then deepen your breath and turn your attention inward. You might close your eyes or have a soft gaze. As you inhale, imagine that you are breathing in the gift of life, being sustained moment by moment by the Spirit, the One who breathes the world alive for generations. As you exhale, let go of any distractions, judgments, or other thoughts that are keeping you from being fully present to this moment.

Allow your breath to drop your awareness from your head, the place of thinking and analyzing, down to your heart, the place of feeling and integration. It is with the heart that we see across the veil. Take a moment to notice what you are feeling right now—not trying to change it, just honoring the truth of your experience and making room for it inside of you.

Remember what the mystics tell us: that the infinite Source of compassion dwells in our hearts. Draw that compassion in, and allow it to fill you.

Call upon the angels and any saints that are especially dear to you to be present with you as you make this inner journey. Ask for their protection in keeping any forces that wish harm to you away.

Begin to feel your ribcage expand around your heart with each breath. In your imagination, become aware of this great chain of being across time that brought you to this moment. Imagine the lives of your parents, then their parents, and their parents. See generations of women and men who lived their lives as best they could, people with deep wounds, carrying grief, longings, desires, and profound moments of joy, celebration, love, and connection. See time unfold behind you like a sacred scroll containing many stories that flow through your blood.

Call to mind one of those ancestors right now—maybe an ancestor you knew well, someone whom you heard stories about, or perhaps an unknown presence—or you might choose a saint who has been significant for you. Speak their name aloud if you know it. Take a few moments to imagine them just beyond the veil. Allow some time to simply be together in the silence.

Notice if their presence feels well and vibrant or shadowy and distant. If the latter, release their presence and come out of the meditation. If the former, open your eyes softly and light a candle, asking this person to be present with you now. Call on this person's support. Is there a particular prayer or desire you want to ask them to support you with? Are you struggling with something in your life? Or perhaps you are in a period of still grieving for the loss of their physical presence and so your prayer might just be for ease and grace in letting go or for a sense of comfort.

Imagine that the presence of this person might be an ally for you now that they have moved into a different form than on earth. You can call on them to bless you and guide you; you have the wisdom of generations available to you.

Take a few moments of silence and ask for a word of wisdom. In the early Christian desert tradition, people would go in search of wise elders and ask for a word to chew on for the days and months to come. The word was often a phrase or image to ponder and integrate. Consider asking your wise elders across the veil for such a word. Pay attention to any images, feelings, or memories that arise.

Remember the whole Communion of Saints. Call to mind this great cloud of witnesses and community of fellow pilgrims who have also loved and lost and wrestled with life's suffering and embraced life's beauty.

Return to your breath, again breathing in the gift of life, breathing out, releasing into this moment.

Let your breath carry you back to the room, and allow some moments for a gentle transition.

Creative Exploration: Creating an Ancestor Shrine

You are invited to create a shrine in honor of one (or more) ancestors. A shrine is essentially a means of remembrance through art. In creating a shrine for a loved one, the most important element is your own prayerful intention and desire to be in relationship to this person. Choose someone with whom you had a healthy and vibrant relationship. This could be an ancestor of blood and bone or of spirit. It doesn't have to be someone you met in person, but perhaps it's someone in the family you always felt connected to because of the stories shared about them. Shrines of remembrance are often created during November, which is the month of the dead, beginning with the feasts of All Saints and All Souls, but remembering your ancestors in this way can be done any time of year.

In preparation, there are some supplies you might want to gather:

- Base structure, such as a cigar box, a wooden box (you can find these at craft stores), a lunchbox, or a key box. Something with a lid or door works well. Consider looking in thrift stores for something interesting to cover with paint or old letters and photos.
- Acrylic paint in a variety of colors you feel drawn to
- Brushes
- Soft acrylic gel medium or decoupage glue (to adhere paper objects to a surface)
- Decorations (feathers, mosaic tiles, jewels, symbols, etc.)
- Craft glue
- Copies of letters, family recipes, maps of ancestral lands, etc.

- Family photos (consider making copies to use)
- Smooth stones (gather one or more)
- Thick permanent marker

You actually don't need very many supplies to create your shrine, and sometimes the best approach is to let things in the world that want to be included come to you. So I suggest not going to the craft store to purchase a whole bunch of things, but discerning what is foundational for the structure and then adding as needed.

Before you begin working, spend some time centering yourself and connecting to your breath. You may want to move through the "Calling on the Ancestors" meditation again as a way of feeling a connection to your ancestors. Reflect on how you want to honor this person. Perhaps light a candle as a way to begin.

Begin with whatever base form you have chosen—a box or structure of some kind. Notice what colors you are feeling drawn to. Try not to plan this out, but enter into an intuitive engagement with the materials, trusting the process as it unfolds. Art-making is in part about getting messy and dwelling in the space of unknowing as the creative process reveals what is next. If you feel stuck, you might step away for a little while or go on a walk outdoors.

Experiment with colors and paint the base. You can always wait for it to dry (or use a hair dryer to speed the process) and paint over it again if desired.

Use the decoupage glue or soft acrylic gel medium to adhere paper to the shrine—photos, old letters, or recipes. You might tear these and use just a piece. You can brush this glue over the surface of the image as well to seal it in. If desired, you can mix it with some paint to give a tint of color.

Use a craft glue to adhere any symbols or natural objects you want on your shrine. These don't need to have a logical rationale for being included. Again, trust your intuition. You might go on a contemplative walk to gather symbols in nature.

When you have completed the process (and you might take several days to work on this), offer a blessing for your shrine; and when it is dry, put it somewhere visible. Spend time with it, and let your creation continue to speak to you.

Closing Blessing

Working with my ancestors has been a significant part of my spiritual journey for the last twenty years. I have gone on many pilgrimages to walk the lands they walked; I have done a lot of genealogical research to see where the threads of my family history lead. But probably most important, I spend time most days in the morning calling in their presence during my time of prayer and meditation. I listen for what guidance they might have for my life. This is a poem I wrote for my motherline:

Ancestral Time

To say their names, an incantation
against loneliness and forgetting:

Suzanne, who fled the suburbs to New York City
birthed one daughter, died too soon

Faith met her love on the Greyhound bus,
fifty years later a slow death from cancer

Marjorie, whose mother died so young
then took passage across the gaping sea

Louisa, divorced 1897, died two years later
records show abuse, desertion

Sarah, a widow cared for her grandchildren
I wish I knew more

then Sarah again, and back to Mary
whose last name I do not even know

perhaps she is the primordial Mary
maybe Eve is there too.

All that remains now of the motherline,
crumbling papers tracing
births, baptisms, marriages, deaths,
census forms with addresses long demolished,
sometimes a ship's manifest shows
escape or freedom.

What seems so long ago breathes
inside us, we live their lives again,
not understanding the long ache
the need for some primal scream
taking us by surprise one
sunny day, until we hear
all their voices flower in the rage,
and sometimes we hear
their whispers in the night
among shadowed kisses,
how thrusting in the dark
brought forth generations.

They speak to us in dreams,
my body a mirror
and their lives faint fingerprints
seen in the morning light
just upon waking.[5]

EIGHT

Cosmic Time

> Time is the measure of things that come to an end, but
> where time itself ends, eternity begins. . . . In the end,
> there is no end. The ends of time are near the roots of
> eternity, and the ends of the Earth touch on the other
> world or the world behind the world.
>
> —Michael Meade, *The World Behind the World*

Despite all of our time-saving tools and gadgets, the truth is we need
less and less conscious attention to complete the tasks of our day. If anything, we are tempted to multitask to get as much done as possible at
one time so we are never truly present to anything we are doing. Jacob
Needleman, in his book *Time and the Soul*, writes that most of us are like
what the Tibetans call "hungry ghosts"—not really existing, not present
to life, obsessed with hurrying and doing things right away: "But *right
away* is the opposite of now—the opposite of the lived *present* moment
in which the passing of time no longer tyrannizes us."[1] He goes on to say
that the hungry ghosts continue to starve by hungering only after a false
illusion of more hours and more days, when what we really hunger for is
the present moment. I recognize that I could live a thousand years, but
if I am not present to it, I will still feel the dissatisfaction and absence of
meaning to the end of my days.

When we feel trapped by having "no time," we have lost touch with
the eternal. Culture reinforces this by always claiming that we are nearing the end of time. Apocalyptic predictions are a part of this larger narrative, and they appear in every era. We feel victimized by our lengthy
to-do lists and day planners. Clearly, we are living in a period of chaos

and decay. When we view time from a linear perspective, we feel as though we are hurtling toward our own untimely ends.

However, organic time, as we have been exploring in this book through rhythms of the sun and moon, is cyclical and sees periods of destruction as making the way for new growth and possibility. Autumn and winter always lead to springtime. When religious traditions write about life after death being eternal, they don't mean that we will live as we do now, only with an endless numbers of days. Instead, we will be immersed in the Now. The purpose of most spiritual practices is to simply arrive right Here, right Now. And for many of us, it will be the longest journey we ever take.

This spiral or cyclical vision of time connects us to a grander order of things, one less concerned with the minute details of each day, with our moments fraught with anxiety or fear of being behind. We have been widening our perspective in this book from breath to day to week to month to year to lifetime. We now take one more giant step back for an even wider perspective.

The Universe as a Great Breath

Thomas Berry wrote in his book *The Great Work: Our Way into the Future*, about the very rhythms we are exploring here:

> If such moments as dawn and dusk, birth and death, and the seasons of the year are such significant moments, how awesome, then, must be the present moment when we witness the dying of the Earth in its Cenozoic expression and the life renewal of the Earth in an emerging Ecozoic Era. . . . We will recover our sense of wonder and our sense of the sacred only if we appreciate the universe beyond ourselves as a revelatory experience of that numinous presence whence all things come into being.[2]

Our current scientific understanding of the universe is that it emerged from the Big Bang, an original moment of fiery explosion sending matter hurtling through space and forming stars. With this comes the awareness that the cosmos is ever-expanding and will one day reach a point of fullness, and then begin to slowly and steadily contract again.

The universe itself is a place where the turning of seasons is at work and we are invited to behold it and see what we discover. This giant cosmic breath of expansion and contraction takes place over billions of years. We are part of a long, elegant, and cosmic breath, one that mirrors the rising and setting of the sun each day, the waxing and waning of the moon, the turning of the earth and her seasons, and the movements of our lives.

Because of the nature of cosmic time extending for millions of years, we can only see ourselves at one point in the cycle, a fleeting moment, rather than moving through the cycles again and again as with the seasons, the moon cycles, or the days of our lives. Somehow, though, these smaller rhythms offer us faith in the larger rhythms at work.

Deep Time

Deep time is geologic time, time considered from the perspective of stone, the formation of mountains, and planetary movements of tectonic plates. Geologist Marcia Bjornerud writes in her book *Timefulness: How Thinking Like a Geologist Can Help Save the World*:

> Fathoming deep time is arguably geology's single greatest contribution to humanity. Just as the microscope and telescope extended our vision into spatial realms once too minuscule or immense for us to see, geology provides a lens through which we can witness time in a way that transcends the limits of our human experience.[3]

She describes those timelines that scale the 4.5 billion-year history of Earth into a twenty-four-hour length and that demonstrate how human beings only appear at a fraction before midnight. But she is critical of how disempowering this model can be, especially given the extent of the damage we have done in our short time here. She writes that the "extended family of living organisms has been around since at least 6 a.m.,"[4] and these are our ancestors as well.

The other issue she has with this model is its linear depiction. There is no future integrated into it. After midnight is an unknown—or worse, it doesn't exist. This isn't how time works, however, as we have seen. Time moves in circles and great cycles, some as intimate as our own breath or the nearness of the day, and some grander, such as the seasons of the year or even those patterns of death and new birth again and again in a lifetime. But even on the cosmic scale, we must believe that the universe is somehow a macrocosm of these microcosms that appear all through our experiences of time.

Mythic Time

Sometimes we might feel as though we are at the end of time, at least on a human scale. News every day of the ever-deepening climate crisis should alarm all of us. I write and edit this book during the pandemic. We might wonder, Is this the true apocalypse? Are we living in the end of days?

Mythologist and storyteller Michael Meade writes, "Tales of apocalyptic endings can be found in most cultures; like stories of creation they are part of the human inheritance of myth and imagination. Endings and beginnings are mythic moments par excellence; they are the extremities of existence and the bookends of cosmology."[5] What some of the great creation myths tell us is that in all endings are also the seeds of a new beginning. We find this in the cycles we have been exploring in this book as well. The seasons of the year move not in a straight line but in a circle, always moving through the release of autumn and rest of winter, emerging into spring's blossoming and summer's fruitfulness.

On a cosmic scale, these cycles may be much longer to see. We may be in the midst of the winter of our humanity, but what myths tell us is that something will eventually break through into blossom. It will likely look nothing like what any of us expects, and it may not be what we would choose. But mythic time encourages us to trust these rhythms. Even the Greek root of the word *apocalypse* means "to reveal what is hidden, to uncover a secret meaning." In the midst of the intensity of life's drama and unfolding, being in a time of endings also means moving toward new beginnings. This time can be when new possibilities and truths are revealed that have until now been hidden.

Michael Meade continues: "To be alive at this time means to become a witness, willing or unwilling, to the loosening of the web of nature as well as the unraveling of the fabric of culture. It means to be present as accepted patterns dissolve, as institutions become hollow and uncertainty comes to rule. . . . The issue is not the literal 'end of the world,' but the winding down and speeding up that happens on the downside of a cosmic cycle."[6] Geology and myth come together to reveal a story of cycles; time always moves in a circle rather than a straight line. Recognizing this is a humbling way of feeling our insignificance in the grand scheme of things while also feeling the importance of our being alive in this moment right now.

Perhaps the more we live into the cyclical rhythms of breath, day, moon, and seasons, the more we might trust that a new story is coming.

How will we be present to the endings in our world? How will we help to cultivate new beginnings?

Scripture Reflection from John Valters Paintner

Six Days of Creation and the Sabbath

(Genesis 1:1–3:24)

In the beginning, when God created the heavens and the earth, the earth was a formless void and darkness covered the face of the deep, while a wind from God swept over the face of the waters. Then God said, "Let there be light"; and there was light. And God saw that the light was good; and God separated the light from the darkness. God called the light Day, and the darkness was called Night. And there was evening and there was morning, the first day. . . .

Thus the heavens and the earth were finished, and all their multitude. And on the seventh day God finished the work that he had done, and rested on the seventh day from all the work that he had done. So God blessed the seventh day and hallowed it, because on it God rested from all the work that he had done in creation.

These are the generations of the heavens and the earth when they were created.

—Genesis 1:1–5, 2:1–4a

Even though it is likely the second of the two biblical creation myths to be written, this story of the six days of creation is the first sequentially in scripture and it's how the Bible begins. It is based on a pre-scientific understanding of the universe, one that had not yet even discovered the wider universe. The cosmology of this myth (as a story of ultimate meaning) is that of a giant, inside-out snow globe. That is, the literal description given is of a large, flat disc covered with a massive dome that keeps the waters of the heavens at bay. But that's not what the story is trying to tell us, and so it doesn't matter that it's scientifically inaccurate.

As the story opens, before God starts creating, there is not nothing. It is not an infinite empty void. No. There is something, and that something is the abyss, a swirling mass of water and wind and chaos. It is a giant storm that best symbolizes the ancient Babylonian fertility god Ba'al (the same one Yahweh routinely defeats in various forms throughout the Hebrew Scriptures and once in the gospel, when Jesus speaks to calm the storm, thus demonstrating his divinity). According to the Babylonians, Ba'al would bless them by bringing the rains so the crops would grow. And Ba'al would also curse them by bringing the storms that would destroy the harvest and drown the livestock. The Babylonians never knew what the ever-fickle Ba'al had in store for them, and the best they could do was to sacrifice crops, animals, and even their own children in hopes to appease this violent and unpredictable god.

Enter Yahweh, who speaks and brings order to the chaos. It's that simple. It's not even a fight, really. Yahweh speaks, and the abyss obeys. Day by day, slowly and efficiently, God creates the world. God separates the waters (the water below the land and the water above the dome of the sky) to make dry land. God makes light and separates it from the darkness (day and night). God makes the plants, fish, insects, birds, animals, and finally humans (man and woman together on the same day in this version of the story) in God's own image. At the end of each day, God declares creation good, and humans are declared very good.

Simply put, God speaks, and the world is created. It is God's divine breath that makes the world and all that fills it. Not only does God form the chaos into order but also the order has a purpose. God makes a pocket in the storm of the abyss and slowly fills it with everything humans will need to survive and flourish. When all is made ready, humans are created in the Divine image as the culmination of all God's work.

The message here at the core of the Judeo-Christian belief system is that God is good and loving and has provided us with everything we need. But unlike the followers of Ba'al who just accepted the world as a cruel and evil place, the Jews had to explain how a good universe would include suffering and death. And that's where the second creation myth comes in, when Adam and Eve (representatives of our core nature) disobey God and break the perfect world (as we discussed in chapter 1). But in that story, we read of how God formed humans from the clay and breathed life into us. Our souls come from God's very breath. We are not only made from creation; we are also infused with the Creator.

I was raised in a religious household. My family was very active in the Catholic Church, and so I grew up with a belief that I was endowed by my Creator with a soul. While I may not always feel particularly spiritual, I always believe there is something within me that connects me to something greater beyond myself. My soul is an unmerited gift from God that connects me to the rest of humanity and all of creation.

But I have some doubts about my physical body. I fit squarely within gender/identity roles that are widely accepted in modern Western society. I don't have any disabilities, although a friend who was born with a disability reminded me recently that we're all just "temporarily abled" and that "disability" has more to do with how we design society than with any perceived physical limitations. But even with my "advantages" (again, due more to how we design society than anything else), I still have issues with my body. I wish I were a bit taller. I wish my knees and eyes weren't beginning to show their age. I know it's stupid and ungrateful, but if I wake up after having slept in an odd position and am stiff or achy, then I don't feel as if I've been made in the Divine image.

The solution to this self-imposed dilemma is to reject the false dualism on which it's based. I'm not a soul riding around in a muscle-powered skeleton. Just as every cell in my body is oxygenated by my breath, every part of my physical self is infused with the breath of the Creator. I may not be society's idea of "a perfect specimen," but God has looked on me and found me very good.

I am not divine. But I am of the Divine. And through that connection to the One who created me, I am connected to the rest of creation. So while I may not be cosmic myself, I am part of the cosmos. I am part of the sacred flow of time, not just of this moment of time. We are all part of sacred time.

How do you find connection with the rest of humanity, creation, and the cosmos?

Practice: Slow Listening

How often do we truly listen to another person when we are having a conversation? Do we focus on our own thoughts and anticipate what we are planning to say next in response, or do we allow ourselves to fully receive what is being shared first before thinking about how to respond? This kind of pure presence to another is a rare gift in a busy world eager to get to the point of things. Most of us will touch this intentional, slow listening only in moments with our loved ones and friends, perhaps at work if we are trained as chaplains or spiritual directors.

For this practice I invite you to find a stone from the area where you live. Do a bit of research on your local geology if you are unsure. How old are the stones? How did they form?

Hold the stone in your palm and listen to it. What does it want to say to you? Can you release your own need to speak or anticipate and just enter into this space of presence together?

One of the great gifts living in Ireland has given me is a profound respect for stone. To the west of us is the granite region of Connemara with its bogs, heather, and lakes. To the south of us is the Burren, a limestone region where the bedrock is exposed and the rock is porous so the water goes underground. The limestone is a compressed tropical seabed that has shifted from the equator over a span of millions of years. These two kinds of stone, granite and limestone, are profoundly different from each other. Living near them reminds me that each has a story to tell.

When I stand in the old stone church ruins, or by a holy well, I can hear the prayers that have been spoken into those stones over generations. They are the keepers of stories and prayers. The stones, whether in nature or part of a building, have so much to tell us.

Meditation: Expanding Rhythms

Begin by getting in a comfortable position and closing your eyes if you feel comfortable doing so. Start to pay attention to your breath without changing anything. Simply take a few moments to connect with this life-sustaining energy moving through you.

Now begin to slow your breath down and move into an awareness of the four parts of the breath—there is the moment of inhale, the pause between your inhale and exhale, the moment of exhale, and the pause between your exhale and inhale. Take a couple of breaths in which you are aware of all four moments in your breath and noticing the different quality each part has. Be present to the experience of rising, fullness, falling, and emptiness. Allow a few moments to experience this.

Then on your next inhale, in your imagination expand your awareness so that you become aware of the hours of the day. Allow each breath to move you through the cycles of dawning, the fullness of day, the descending of dusk, and the darkness of night. Move through several breath cycles holding this in your heart. What do you notice as you move through the rise and fall of each day? Where are the moments you feel a longing to pause? Imagine the great tides drawing in and out each day.

On your next inhale expand your awareness so that you become aware of the rhythms of the week. Imagine yourself moving through the tasks of your days as a time of fullness. Then imagine yourself releasing into the grace of Sabbath as a time of renewing for the work ahead. Then move back into the work of the week with the renewal that comes from tasting eternity.

Then expand your awareness further so that you bring the cycles of the moon into your imagination. With each breath cycle, inhale and imagine the waxing of the moon, then her fullness; with the exhale imagine the moon's waning, then her embrace of darkness. Allow some time to be present to this experience.

Taking another deep breath, let your awareness expand again to imagine the seasons of the year. Move through them with each breath—the blossoming of spring, the fullness and heat of summer, the harvest and releasing of autumn, and the hibernation of winter. Rest for a few moments with this awareness.

Continue to breathe deeply and expand your imagination to the cycle of your life. Notice as you move through your breath cycle if any memories, awareness, or insight comes to you. What is the season you are in now? What is the season you are moving toward? Stay here for a few moments, being present to the rise and fall of your life experience.

Expand to an even wider circle and imagine embracing all of your ancestors behind you. See the way the love of thousands has brought you into this life in this moment of time. Breathe gratitude for their struggles and endurance, their love and witness.

Expand your awareness once again, and call to mind Teilhard de Chardin's image of "the breathing together of all things." See yourself as intimately connected to all of creation in a great rhythm of expansion and contraction. Imagine the trees taking in the carbon dioxide you release, transforming it into oxygen, and then sending out oxygen for you to take in and nourish yourself, all in an endless dance. Imagine all of the creatures breathing in harmony with you.

Expand your vision one more time, and see yourself as a part of the great cosmos that scientists tell us emerges from a Big Bang, a moment of powerful explosion, and over millions of years expands and expands into the universe, until one day when there will be a tipping point and everything will contract again, as in one great cosmic breath of which we are a tiny part.

Bring your attention back to this moment. Slowly and gently return to your normal breath pattern, and simply notice how your body is feeling. Allow some time to journal about anything you discovered.

Creative Exploration: Bask in the Presence of the Cosmos

For much of our human history, a relationship to the sky has been essential. We knew the time of day by the position of the sun. We knew which direction to travel by the stars. When we created patterns in the sky known as constellations, we infused the night sky with a mythological meaning. We have largely lost our connection to these ancient stories, which would have given ancient peoples a sense of their place among things.

When we are lost we turn to our GPS devices, which in turn refer to a set of artificial satellites orbiting the sky. Knowing where we are in the world is essential to understanding who we are, yet what happens when our position in the world shifts from the constellations to the satellites? From the magnificent mystery of the cosmos to human-created objects?

If the weather in your part of the world allows it, find time to stand under the night sky. Allow some time just to stand in awe under this canopy of stars. Take in what you can see and connect to your breath, knowing that the cosmos participates in this breath cycle as well. Open yourself to this perspective of cosmic time, of your own smallness in the face of such vastness. See if you might breathe this in as a gift of freedom, of recognizing how the small things that make us so anxious are held in context of the creation of a universe. Notice your own body's response.

Consider a movement exploration in which you move between these intimate cycles of your own breath rising and falling and a contemplation of the vastness of the universe. Remember what Michael Meade writes about how all myth moves in circles, where the beginning emerges from the ending again and again. This can be as simple as expanding and contracting your arms, widening them into the space around you and then drawing them close to you.

Let your body inhabit this great rhythm on a personal and cosmic level, and see what you notice as you remember the night sky and that you too are made from stardust.

You can take this experience into a "gush art" experience, which is spontaneous and intuitive drawing. Using simple materials such as colored markers, pencils, or crayons and some blank paper, give yourself time to play. Draw the colors that are calling to you. See how you might express this cosmic rhythm on paper, knowing you will never capture it all but that you can allow an expression of it in this moment.

When you are done, allow some time to process the experience with some journaling.

Closing Blessing

As we cultivate a new relationship to time—one rooted in presence to this moment, one that honors the various seasons of textures of time and how it always moves in circles—we can perhaps deepen in our trust of the divine unfolding of things. We can hopefully begin to lay aside some of our own fears and anxieties, our rush to get somewhere important or to do important things. We might breathe more, pausing more often just to savor and linger over life's splendid moments.

What have you discovered in this journey? What have been the challenges and the graces?

Cosmos

That first moment,
explosion of fire and fury
a stampede of suns
light poured into the dark
chalice of space
sparks wheel across
the dome overhead.

We look to the inky sky
to track creatures formed there,
crab and scorpion, lion and bear
stars which died a million years ago
still throbbing with impossible light.

When I close my eyes
I see them still and it seems
they reach to me and I to them.
Is it gravity, or a longing kindled
by stardust within me
or the doorway to forever?[7]

Conclusion

Value of time is not in time but in clarity of thought: the moments when we see through time and everything else, and see our way "through" everything. Time is valuable only for the moments that cut across and through it vertically.

—Thomas Merton, *Learning to Love*

I remember one day while I was living in Seattle, as I was driving to my yoga class, a footrace was blocking all of the cross-streets I usually travel. I finally found my way around it, but at that point I was close to being late and so started to feel a bit agitated with stoplights and slow drivers in front of me. I could hear the voices start in my mind: *Hurry up! If you don't get there early . . .*

"What?" I interrupted myself. "I won't get my favorite spot in the room? They'll lock the door when class begins and I won't get in?" While those both may have been true, the irony of my rushing impatiently to yoga class sank in, and I took a deep breath and let the spaciousness of the moment fill me. Worrying wasn't going to get me to class any faster, and I would instead be more likely to get into an accident.

I would like to say that this kind of scene plays itself out very rarely in my life, but I would be trying to convince you that I am not susceptible to being very human. The same thing happens when I have too many deadlines and I feel the pressure of too many things to do in too little time. And while I find myself caught in the inner dialogue about time often, I have become more adept at catching myself in these moments.

How many of us wish there were more hours in the day to get things done? As if thirty-hour days or being able to get by on less sleep would somehow solve our problems with feeling so rushed and busy all the

time. We think that by hurrying we will somehow catch up, but that is
the great illusion.

We are all suffering from time poverty in a culture that worships productivity and accomplishments. We become hostage to our calendars.
In his book *Time Wars*, Jeremy Rifkin says, "We have surrounded ourselves with time-saving technological gadgetry, only to be overwhelmed
by plans that cannot be carried out, appointments that cannot be honored, schedules that cannot be fulfilled, and deadlines that cannot be
met."[1] What is the purpose of managing our days more efficiently if we
don't understand the *meaning* of our days?

There is, of course, the social and cultural reality that many people
are forced to work relentlessly in low-paying jobs, sometimes multiple
jobs to make ends meet. They may not have the ability to create a more
spacious way of living. We need to ask questions about social justice
and demand reforms that will enable people to have a higher quality of
life. Those of us who do have more spacious ways of living accessible
to us have a responsibility to witness to another way of being. Part of
transforming the culture is embodying a different path so others might
see what is possible and, when doable, make this same path available to
them.

In 2010 at Christmas, I had an experience of confronting my own
mortality in a very intimate way. I ended up with a pulmonary embo-
lism after a long-haul flight. It was profound for me to walk away alive
but knowing it could so very easily have been otherwise. I was humbled
and profoundly grateful. As with many others who have had near-death
experiences, the days, weeks, and years since have cultivated in me an
even deeper cherishing of my moments. That experience was a significant part of what compelled me to finally consider moving to Europe,
something I had longed to do for most of my adult life.

And yet the irony is that while I am keenly aware of the precious-
ness of my days and even my hours, overall I don't generally feel more
rushed in my life or more compelled to get things done faster. Instead, I
am compelled to inhabit my days more fully so that each one feels more
like a wide expanse and an open field of possibility rather than a narrow
tunnel nearing its end.

This is the heart of our relationship to time: First, we experience its cyclical rhythms so that we aren't rushing toward deadlines and the end of things but instead always moving toward new beginnings as well. Second, we experience a more expansive and present way of being in the world, where we might touch and taste eternity more often. Eternity is not something that happens after we die; eternity also exists here in all the glorious spaces where we lose track of time because our hearts are so full of wonder and delight. God is a God of circles and rhythms, inviting us always to fall fully into this moment.

Notes

Introduction

1. Mihaly Csikszentmihalyi, *Flow: The Psychology of Optimal Experience* (New York: Harper & Row, 1990), 75.

2. Gary Eberle, *Sacred Time and the Search for Meaning* (Boston: Shambhala, 2003), 7.

3. Eberle, *Sacred Time and the Search for Meaning*, 8.

4. Christian McEwen, *World Enough and Time: Creativity and Slowing Down* (Peterborough, NH: Bauhan Publishing, 2011), Kindle version.

5. McEwen, *World Enough and Time*.

6. Juliet Schor, "Work Less, Live More," *Yes!* Fall 2011 issue, https://www.yesmagazine.org/issue/jobs/2011/09/02/less-work-more-living/.

7. Jay Griffiths, *A Sideways Look at Time* (New York: Penguin, 2004), 29.

8. Josef Pieper, *In Tune with the World: A Theory of Festivity* (South Bend, IN: St. Augustine's Press, 1965), 19.

1. The Breath

1. Teilhard de Chardin, quoted in Esther de Waal, *The Celtic Way of Prayer: The Recovery of the Religious Imagination* (New York: Image Books, 1997), xv.

2. David Abram, *The Spell of the Sensuous* (New York: Random House, 1997), 246.

3. Mary Oliver, "Have You Ever Tried to Enter the Long Black Branches?" in *West Wind: Poems and Prose Poems* (New York: Houghton Mifflin, 1997), 62.

4. Hildegard of Bingen, quoted in booklet for *Feather on the Breath of God: Sequences and Hymns by Abbess Hildegard of Bingen*, Hyperion Records, 1985, compact disc.

5. Jean-Yves Leloup, *Being Still: Reflections on an Ancient Mystical Tradition* (New York: Paulist Press, 2003), 75.

6. Christine Valters Paintner, *The Wisdom of the Body: A Contemplative Journey to Wholeness for Women* (Notre Dame, IN: Sorin Books, 2017), 41.

7. Christine Valters Paintner, *Dreaming of Stones* (Brewster, MA: Paraclete Press, 2019), 25.

2. Rhythms of the Day

1. Macrina Wiederkehr, *Seven Sacred Pauses: Living Mindfully through the Hours of the Day* (Notre Dame, IN: Ave Maria Press, 2010).

2. David Steindl-Rast, *Music of Silence: A Sacred Journey through the Hours of the Day* (Berkeley, CA: Ulysses Press, 2001), 4.

3. Both Universalis.com and DivineOffice.org offer resources to support you in praying the Hours.

4. I first encountered this way of naming the four primary Hours in Kathleen Deignan's *Book of Hours* (Notre Dame, IN: Ave Maria Press, 2007), which draws on quotes from Thomas Merton about prayer.

5. Northumbria Community Trust, *Celtic Daily Prayer* (New York: HarperCollins, 2000), 152.

6. *Rule of St. Benedict* 73.8.

7. Jalâluddîn Rumi, "Say Yes Quickly," trans. Coleman Barks, in *Open Secret* (Boston: Shambhala, 1999), 7.

8. Gabriele Uhlein, *Meditations with Hildegard of Bingen* (Rochester, VT: Inner Traditions / Bear & Co., 1983), 128.

9. Steindl-Rast, *Music of Silence*, 96–97.

10. Wendell Berry, *New Collected Poems* (Berkeley, CA: Counterpoint, 2013), 121.

11. Christine Valters Paintner, *Dreaming of Stones* (Brewster, MA: Paraclete Press, 2019), 26.

3. Weekly Rhythms and Sabbath Rest

1. Abraham Joshua Heschel, *The Sabbath* (New York: Farrar Giroux Straus, 2005), 3.

2. Chronobiology is the study of how living beings respond to time.

3. Walter Brueggemann, *Sabbath as Resistance* (Louisville, KY: Westminster John Knox Press, 2017), Kindle edition.

4. Marva J. Dawn, *Keeping the Sabbath Wholly: Ceasing, Resting, Embracing, Feasting* (Grand Rapids, MI: Eerdmans, 1989), 3.

5. Thomas Merton, *Conjectures of a Guilty Bystander* (New York: Image Classic, 1968), 81.

6. Christine Valters Paintner, *Dreaming of Stones* (Brewster, MA: Paraclete Press, 2019), 27.

4. Waxing and Waning Lunar Cycles

1. Peter London, *Drawing Closer to Nature: Making Art in Dialogue with the Natural World* (Boston: Shambhala, 2003), 201.

2. Christine Valters Paintner, *Dreaming of Stones* (Brewster, MA: Paraclete Press, 2019), 28.

5. Seasons of the Year

1. Sean O'Duinn, *Where Three Streams Meet: Celtic Spirituality* (Dublin: Columba Books, 2000).

2. *Rule of Benedict*, 4:47.

3. Wallace Stevens, "It Must Be Abstract," in *The Collected Poems of Wallace Stevens* (New York: Vintage International, 2015), 408.

4. *Scripture of Leaves* is the title of one of William Stafford's poetry collections.

5. Christine Valters Paintner, *Dreaming of Stones* (Brewster, MA: Paraclete Press, 2019), 29.

6. Seasons of a Lifetime

1. Christine Valters Paintner, *Dreaming of Stones* (Brewster, MA: Paraclete Press, 2019), 30.

7. Ancestral Time

1. Carl Jung, *Memories, Dreams, Reflections* (New York: Vintage Books, 1989), 233–34.

2. Michael Meade, *Fate and Destiny: The Two Agreements of the Soul* (Housatonic, MA: Green Fire Press, 2012).

3. Roberta Gilbert, *The Eight Concepts of Bowen Theory* (Lake Frederick, VA: Leading Systems Press, 2018).

4. Phil Cousineau, *The Art of Pilgrimage: The Seeker's Guide to Making Travel Sacred* (San Francisco: Conari Press, 1998), xxix.

5. Christine Valters Paintner, *Dreaming of Stones* (Brewster, MA: Paraclete Press, 2019), 31.

8. Cosmic Time

1. Jacob Needleman, *Time and the Soul: Where Has All the Meaningful Time Gone and Can We Get It Back?* (Oakland, CA: Berrett-Koehler Publishers, 2003), 10.

2. Thomas Berry, *The Great Work: Our Way into the Future* (New York: Crown Publishing, 2000), 49.

3. Marcia Bjornerud, *Timefulness: How Thinking Like a Geologist Can Help Save the World* (Princeton, NJ: Princeton University Press, 2018), 16.

4. Bjornerud, *Timefulness*, 17.

5. Michael Meade, *Why the World Doesn't End: Tales of Renewal in Times of Loss* (Housatonic, MA: Green Fire Press, 2008), Kindle edition.

6. Meade, *Why the World Doesn't End*.

7. Christine Valters Paintner, *Dreaming of Stones* (Brewster, MA: Paraclete Press, 2019), 33.

Conclusion

1. Jeremy Rifkin, *Time Wars: The Primary Conflict in Human History* (New York: Touchstone Books, 1989), 12, quoted in Jacob Needleman, *Time and the Soul: Where Has All the Meaningful Time Gone and Can We Get It Back?* (Oakland, CA: Berrett-Koehler Publishers, 2003), 19.

Christine Valters Paintner is the online abbess for Abbey of the Arts, a virtual monastery offering classes and resources on contemplative practice and creative expression. She earned a doctorate in Christian spirituality from the Graduate Theological Union in Berkeley, California, and achieved professional status as a registered expressive arts consultant and educator from the International Expressive Arts Therapy Association. She is also trained as a spiritual director and supervisor.

Paintner is the author of fifteen books on monasticism and creativity, including *Earth, Our Original Monastery*; *The Soul's Slow Ripening*; *Water, Wind, Earth, and Fire*; *The Artist's Rule*; *The Soul of a Pilgrim*; *Illuminating the Way*; *The Wisdom of the Body*; and two collections of poetry. She is a Benedictine oblate living in Galway, Ireland, with her husband, John. Together they lead writing retreats and pilgrimages in Ireland, Scotland, Austria, and Germany, as well as online retreats at their website AbbeyoftheArts.com.

abbeyofthearts.com
Facebook: @AbbeyoftheArts
Instagram: @abbeyofthearts
Twitter: @abbeyofthearts

ALSO BY
CHRISTINE
VALTERS PAINTNER

The Artist's Rule
Nurturing Your Creative Soul with Monastic Wisdom

Earth, Our Original Monastery
Cultivating Wonder and Gratitude through Intimacy with Nature

Eyes of the Heart
Photography as a Christian Contemplative Practice

Illuminating the Way
Embracing the Wisdom of Monks and Mystics

The Soul of a Pilgrim
Eight Practices for the Journey Within

The Soul's Slow Ripening
12 Celtic Practices for Seeking the Sacred

Water, Wind, Earth, and Fire
The Christian Practice of Praying with the Elements

The Wisdom of the Body
A Contemplative Journey to Wholeness for Women